Treatise on Divine Predestination

NOTRE DAME TEXTS IN MEDIEVAL CULTURE

Vol. 5

The Medieval Institute
University of Notre Dame

John Van Engen, Editor

JOHN SCOTTUS ERIUGENA

Treatise on Divine Predestination

Translated by Mary Brennan

with an Introduction to the English translation by
Avital Wohlman

UNIVERSITY OF NOTRE DAME PRESS
Notre Dame, Indiana

University of Notre Dame Press
Copyright © 1998 by University of Notre Dame
Notre Dame, Indiana 46556
www.undpress.nd.edu
All Rights Reserved

Published in the United States of America

Paperback published in 2002

Reprinted in 2009

Library of Congress Cataloging-in-Publication Data
Erigena, Johannes Scotus, ca. 810–ca. 877.
 [De divina praedestinatione liber. English]
 Treatise on divine predestination / John Scottus Eriugena ; translated by Mary Brennan ; with an introduction to the English translation by Avital Wohlman.
  p. cm. — (Notre Dame texts in medieval culture ; v.5)
 Includes bibliographical references.
 ISBN: 0-268-04207-1 (cloth : alk. paper)
 ISBN 13: 978-0-268-04221-9 (pbk. : alk. paper)
 ISBN 10: 0-268-04221-7 (pbk. : alk. paper)
  1. Predestination—Early works to 1800. I. Title. II. Series: Notre Dame texts in medieval culture; vol.5
BT810.2.E7513 1998
234'.9—dc21   98-17148

∞*This book is printed on acid-free paper.*

Contents

Foreword Mary Brennan	ix
Introduction to the English Translation Avital Wohlman	xv
Preface	3
ONE That Every Question Is Solved by the Fourfold System of the Four Rules of the Whole of Philosophy	7
TWO From the Argument of Necessity It Is Concluded That There Cannot Be Two Predestinations	11
THREE Reason Does Not Permit of Two Predestinations	17
FOUR The One, True and Only Predestination of God	25
FIVE No One Is Compelled to Do Good or to Do Evil by the Foreknowledge and Predestination of God	33

Contents

SIX
Every Sin Has No Other Source Than the Free Choice
of the Individual Will   41

SEVEN
Free Choice of the Will Should Be Reckoned among the Good
Things That God Bestows on Man, although He May Misuse It.
What Is It That Causes Sin and Is Sin?   45

EIGHT
The Difference between Man's Nature and His Free Choice   51

NINE
Foreknowledge and Predestination Are Predicated of God,
Not Properly but by a Similitude of Temporal Things   59

TEN
When God Is Said to Know in Advance and to Predestine Sins
or Death or the Punishments of Men or Angels, It Is to Be
Understood from the Contrary   65

ELEVEN
It Can Be Established by Divine and Human Authority
That God's Predestination Concerns Only Those Who Are
Prepared for Eternal Happiness   71

TWELVE
The Definition of Predestination   77

THIRTEEN
What Can Be Inferred from the above Judgment
of Saint Augustine   83

FOURTEEN
Collected Attestations of Saint Augustine by Which It Is
Clearly Proved That There Is but One Predestination
and It Refers Only to the Saints   87

FIFTEEN
By What Kind of Expressions God Is Said to Have Foreknowledge
of Sins since They Are Nothing, or to Predestine the
Punishments of Them Which Likewise Are Nothing   93

SIXTEEN
No Nature Punishes Nature and the Punishments of Sinners
Are Nothing Other Than Their Sins   101

SEVENTEEN
Why God Is Said to Have Predestined Punishments although
He Neither Makes nor Predestines Them   111

Contents

EIGHTEEN
The Error of Those Whose Thinking on Predestination Disagrees with That of the Holy Fathers Has Grown Out of an Ignorance of the Liberal Arts   117

NINETEEN
Eternal Fire   125

Epilogue: Divine Predestination   129

Bibliography   131

Foreword

The *Treatise on Predestination* is the earliest attested work of John Scottus, known as Eriugena.* Even if it had in past centuries generally been studied by way of a gloss to his later great work *Periphyseon (On the Division of Nature)*, it has received considerable attention in recent years from scholars who would appear to regard it rather as a precursor to that work. The present translation is based on Goulven Madec's edition to serve those who may not have access to the Latin text, and it is hoped that it may serve as an instrument for continuing investigation of the text. This introduction does not aim to make that investigation but briefly to outline the circumstances under which the treatise was composed.

Eriugena is known to have lived in France between the years 845 and 877, for the most part at the court of Charles (II) the Bald, grandson of Charlemagne, who was a considerable patron of scholars and artists. He was acknowledged as being of Irish birth, but the date of his birth and the time and circumstances of his arrival in France are unknown. One might surmise that he was born in the first quarter of the ninth century: by 850

---

* The remarks in this Foreword will not be annotated. Readers are referred to the select bibliography provided below and in particular: C. Lambot (1945), J. Devisse (1975), G. Madec (1978), M. Brennan (1986), J. O'Meara (1988) and D. Moran (1989), and, most recently, *Eriugena: East and West* edited by B. McGinn and W. Otten (Notre Dame, 1994).

his reputation as a gifted teacher of the Liberal Arts was well established. In that year he was invited with some urgency by Hincmar, Archbishop of Rheims, and Pardulus, Bishop of Laon, possibly at the king's suggestion, to provide them with a reasoned refutation of the heretical teachings on predestination expounded by Gottschalk, a priest of Orbais in the diocese of Soissons, which came within the jurisdiction of Rheims. Gottschalk had already been condemned and severely censured by a synod at Mainz in 848 and again by a synod at Quierzy in 849, resulting in his imprisonment in the abbey of Hautvillers until his death in 868. From Hautvillers, later in 849, he issued a further and lengthier confirmation (*Confessio prolixior*) of his teaching.

Gottschalk had been accused of teaching that God's predestination applied in two ways, to some men for good, to some for bad. It was the social irresponsibility implicit in such a doctrine, as much as its theological difficulty, that alarmed the ecclesiastical custodians of the Christian state so recently consolidated by Charlemagne. On the other hand, Gottschalk seemed pastorally committed to the propagation of his controversial thesis: his own pathetic experiences may well explain his preoccupation with and continuing speculation upon the question of predestination. When Rabanus Maurus of Mainz activated the first condemnation and returned the offender to his metropolitan, Hincmar, the latter was to discover that the theologians to whom he appealed, such as the abbots Lupus of Ferrières and Ratramnus of Corbie, offered little to controvert the views of Gottschalk, while Prudentius, the bishop of Troyes, appeared to side with Gottschalk.

It was at this juncture that Eriugena, a scholar 'of no ecclesiastical rank,' was called in. His intervention, in which, in fulfilment of his commission, he conscientiously assumes the role of champion of the church and castigator of Gottschalk, left Hincmar further abashed, not alone by its content, but because Eriugena immediately became the object of scurrilous denunciation by Hincmar's fellow prelates, particularly those of the diocese of Lyon. Eriugena appears to have stood aside from further confrontation and, as the controversy dragged on throughout the decade, Hincmar did not again advert to Eriugena's contribution. The state of the question came up again at Quierzy in 853 and at Valence in 855, where Eriugena's 'nineteen chapters,' inelegantly described (echoing Saint Jerome) as 'Irish porridge,' were condemned; there were further deliberations at Langres and at Savonnières in 859 and finally at Douzy in 860

Foreword

when accord was reached on a formula applicable to pastoral needs and acceptable to all shades of supposedly Augustinian persuasion. For this was, of course, a revival of the old argument between Augustine and Pelagius, between extremes of dependence on God's grace on the one hand and on man's free will on the other. Gottschalk thought to base his argument on Augustine; Eriugena thought to refute him from Augustine. Other participants have been described as being poorly versed in Augustine. Eriugena's intervention, *De divina praedestinatione liber*, consists of explanatory preface, nineteen chapters and concluding summary. It could be, and evidently for many centuries was, dismissed as a single document within a much lengthier dossier: the text from which the present translation was made is based on a single ninth-century manuscript, now Paris Bibliothèque nationale, MS lat. 13386, originally from Saint-Germain-des-Prés and of Corbie provenance; the folios form part of a larger manuscript but the condition of the first and last folio indicate an earlier independent existence. Its two earlier editors, in the seventeenth and nineteenth centuries, advised caution on the part of the reader.

Some of the resentment the treatise aroused when first circulated was due simply to its originality. Eriugena appears to have offered no response to his vilification by his critics. Such otherworldly detachment, which should not be construed as coldness, is also a feature of this as of his later writing. He is writing, if one may express it so, from God's point of view. His writing does not, except perhaps by way of often colourful metaphor, take much account of this present life: the preoccupation of predestination is, after all, with a happiness or unhappiness beyond this life. But Augustine had written in this vein. What was new in the ninth century was the challenge thrown out to the accepted mode of theological argument. The dialectical method announced in Eriugena's first chapter was received with a sense of wonder by his first readers, causing pleasure to some and in turn outrage to others. Reason (*ratio*) is given a hearing on an equal footing with the time-honoured authorities (*auctoritates*) of Scripture and the Fathers; this balancing of reason and authority was to be greatly elaborated in the *Periphyseon*. The secular language of the liberal arts is applied in theological discussion, a procedure duly and formally anathematised by Prudentius of Troyes and Florus of Lyon in their rebuttal.

Eriugena's treatise may still be read in the immediate context in which it was written, that is at the request of Hincmar and Pardulus, in the year 850–851, with the intention of controverting the alarming pronouncements of Gottschalk on a *gemina praedestinatio*. However, increasing familiarity with its text leaves one less concerned with its value or otherwise within the ninth-century predestinarian controversy (which was ultimately inconclusive) than with its significance within the body of Eriugena's own writings. It was on the basis of his reputation as a scholar and teacher of the liberal arts that the two prelates invited him to formulate a refutation of Gottschalk's heretical views. The text itself, in its occasionally extravagant vocabulary, indicates how earnestly he seems to have sought to echo their condemnation: it is probable, indeed, that Pardulus of Laon was a close friend of Eriugena. It might be understandable that emphasis has largely tended to be placed on Eriugena's advocacy of the *artes* as an instrument of truth in matters sacred as well as secular: indeed this statement of intent in his first chapter was what particularly incensed his contemporary critics. In addition, the lengthy and recurrent passages from Augustine adduced by Eriugena to controvert Gottschalk's citations from other Augustinian texts, can cast the author from time to time in the role of simply a compiler and deflect one's attention altogether from Eriugena towards a consideration of the development of Augustine's thought. Eriugena's treatment of these sources intermittently called down the wrath of the ninth to the nineteenth and even the twentieth century upon him and has tended to concentrate attention in that direction to the exclusion, perhaps, of other considerations.

The 'hellenising' phase in the development of Eriugena's thought was for long regarded as dating from the point, later in the same decade, at which Charles the Bald is thought to have requested him to translate from the Greek the works of the Pseudo-Dionysius, believed at that time to be the convert of Saint Paul of Acts 17 but accepted now as probably a sixth-century author, still unidentified, whose writing was deeply influenced by Neoplatonism. Scholars of the later half of this present century have questioned the easy assumption that it was the king's assignment which first introduced Eriugena to Greek patristic and philosophical authors; they suggest very reasonably that it may have been his known interest in, and perhaps familiarity with certain writers in that language that occasioned the commission from Charles. On the other hand, one need look no farther than the *Index auctorum* to G. Madec's edition to be reminded that his pedagogic activities would have familiarised him with Greek thought mediated particularly by the Latin writers of late antiquity: one might suggest, for example, the works of Boethius as a fruitful source of this

Foreword

transmitted thought. Thus alongside the parade of dialectical pyrotechnics which constitute Eriugena's argument against Gottschalk there is constantly to be found a barely latent strain of quasi-mystical negative argument which does not always derive from his named 'authorities', Augustine and Scripture. It was this eccentric departure from the accepted mode of theological disputation that disturbed his contemporary critics, just as what they regarded as his ill-concealed Pelagianism and his sacralisation of the *artes* so greatly offended them.

After the first chapter, in which he announces his proposed method of argument, Eriugena provides chapter headings which are some indication of the content of his treatise. These headings refer to such topics as Necessity, Reason, Free Choice of the Will, Man's Nature, the 'inappropriate' attribution of *Fore*knowledge to God, Argument by Contrariety, Predestination to Happiness, the Nothingness of Sin and of Punishment, with a final chapter on Eternal Fire. It is clear that the writings of Saint Augustine loom large in this treatise. Gottschalk had confronted his readers with a certain view of Augustine; Eriugena, while seeking to refute him, wrestles towards a reconciliation of those irrefutably Augustinian statements with others in which he describes Augustine as speaking *a contrario*, defending them by adducing copious examples of such usage in Scripture. This procedure his critics considered nothing less than mischievous, and equally it caused embarrassment to his ecclesiastical friends. Prudentius of Troyes, who formed part of the scholarly circle attached to the ambulant court of Charles the Bald, wrote a sometimes virulent treatise in response, finding himself obliged to abandon the role of friend for that of critic. On the other hand the same critics complained of the respect and acclaim which continued to be accorded to Eriugena, for, aside from Prudentius, one must assume that there were those, including Charles the Bald himself, who were sympathetic to the implication of his arguments. And if nowadays one considers these chapter headings in relation to the great themes addressed by Eriugena in the *Periphyseon*, one must be struck by the emergence, in this early work, not merely of those themes but also of that same persistent passion which motivates his great philosophic synthesis; for in the *Periphyseon* he will, with the aid of *ratio*, attempt a more daring reconciliation, this time of the tenets of Neoplatonism with those of Christianity.

One cannot say whether or not Charles the Bald's invitation to translate the books of the pseudoDionysius might possibly have predated the

Foreword

composition of Eriugena's *De divina praedestinatione liber*; nor can one say whether or not it was Eriugena's final declaration that Predestination is God and is only in 'the things that are' and has no connection at all with 'the things that are not' that inspired his scholarly colleague Wulfad, later bishop of Bourges, to encourage and to some extent assist him, as Eriugena warmly acknowledged, in the composition of the *Periphyseon*, or *Division of Nature*, which takes within its scope, as its opening words proclaim, all the things that are and those that are not.

With regard to the present text: Eriugena found himself able to educe from the writings of Augustine a view of man's destiny that was extraordinarily optimistic. His final chapter (chapter 19) expresses an optimistically benign view of eternal fire. His crowning argument is, however, to be found in chapter 15 in which he strongly asserts the simplicity of God's nature.

I am greatly indebted to Professor John O'Meara, formerly professor of Latin at University College, Dublin, and to Rev. Professor Thomas Finan, Professor of Latin at St. Patrick's College, Maynooth, for their valuable advice and assistance.

Mary Brennan
Dublin

Introduction to the English Translation

Avital Wohlman

Jean Trouillard has contended that Scottus Eriugena or John the Scot was the only authentic Neoplatonist in whom the Latin world could take pride,[1] the only one who knew how to "recover, beyond Saint Augustine, the authentic spirit of Neoplatonism."[2] Affirmations of this sort, however, may not prove the best argument to attract a large audience for this new translation of *De praedestinatione*, for Neoplatonism is often accused of failing to grasp the proper worth of the world in which we live, indeed to be estranged from full-blooded interplay.

As I have tried to show elsewhere, reservations of this sort with regard to Neoplatonism in general and Scottus Eriugena's thought in particular, are quite without foundation.[3] It may be that by reflecting on the role

---

1. J. Trouillard, "Rencontre du néoplatonisme," *Revue de théologie et philosophie* 22 (1972): 9.
2. J. Trouillard, "La *virtus gnostica* selon Jean Scot Erigène," *Revue de théologie et philosophie* 33 (1983): 331.
3. A. Wohlman, *L'homme, le monde sensible et le péché dans la philosophie de Jean Scot Erigène* (Paris, 1987).

Introduction to the English Translation

which *De praedestinatione* played in the real debates of its time we could be liberated from such lack of appreciation.

When John the Scot was charged by Hincmar in 851 to refute the errors of Gottschalk, his reputation as a learned person had already been established. This was during the time when the bishop of Laon, Pardulus, in presenting him to the clergy of Lyons, had identified him as "the famous Irishman at the court."[4] Whatever his experience in Ireland may have been, it was on his arrival in Gaul around 847 that he displayed the depth and variety of his knowledge. He quickly gained the interest and respect of the king, Charles the Bald, by his study and in teaching at the cathedral school of Laon, then one of the intellectual centers of the kingdom.

The Gottschalk, whose writings he had been asked to assess, was a Saxon monk of a noble family, whose father, Count Bruno, had entrusted him as an oblate to the monastery of Fulda, where Hrabanus Maurus would soon be abbot and master of studies. In fact, the career of Gottschalk, both monastic and theological, was marked by controversy. He revolted against the authority of Hrabanus Maurus and sought to be dispensed from his vows. By a series of canonical maneuvers he managed to get himself transferred to Orbais and then to Corbie. This lack of monastic stability was surely a consequence of his doctrinal obstinacy. In an effort to justify his thesis on predestination, whose rigorous character upset many theologians of the time, he undertook long trips without ecclesiastical permission, even to Rome, but especially to the court of Count Eberhard of Friuli, during the years 845–46. As a result of these peregrinations he was finally interned as a prisoner in the monastery of Hautvillers, under the surveillance of Hincmar, at the explicit behest of Hrabanus Maurus, now archbishop of Mainz. His theology of predestination, which he keenly defended despite condemnations and warnings, elicited a passionate and confused debate in the ninth-century church, into which Scottus Eriugena was introduced, however imprudently, by Hincmar of Rheims. As we shall see, he took home more bitterness than renown from this controversy.

Let us note from the outset that the two protagonists in this debate, Gottschalk and John the Scot, were each, in their own way, outsiders to the established order. One was a rebellious monk and a controversial

---

4. Pardulus, "Epistola ad ecclesiam Lugdunensem" inserted in "De tribus epistolis," *PL* 121.1052A.

Introduction to the English Translation

theologian, because he had suffered at the hands of that order. The other, an intellectual and humanist, considered himself beyond its grasp, protected as he was by King Charles. It should also be noted that both of them had access to libraries where they could study classical authors and the church fathers, particularly Augustine, who were by their own account their sole teachers.

Perhaps it was their status as outsiders to the established order which allowed these two thinkers to consider the question of predestination—one of those which elicited most passion in the third generation of the Carolingian Renaissance—in so highly personal a fashion. Indeed, the vehement reactions to their writings showed that they succeeded in disturbing the intellectual harmony Charles the Bald had sought to promote.

We shall begin this introduction by briefly recalling places and settings, as well as the principal personages and ideas which comprised the context of this period of the Carolingian Renaissance. Next we shall study the unfolding of the controversy on predestination and finally see how peace was restored among minds at the price of a compromise between two theologically opposed visions of the relationship between divine knowledge and human freedom.

The Third Generation of the Carolingian Renaissance

The term 'renaissance' has long been reserved for the explosion of arts and letters which characterized the sixteenth century. According to a tenacious prejudice, the Renaissance appeared as a sudden dawn putting an end to the prolonged darkness of the Middle Ages. Studies appearing in recent decades, however, have shown just how simplistic such a vision has been. We have discovered, with increasing amazement, that the Middle Ages were marked by successive renaissances which progressively shaped humanism in the West. Chronologically, the first of these renaissances is what we have called the Carolingian Renaissance, named after the emperor who initiated it in the ninth century. Under the authority and the stimulus of Charlemagne, western Europe experienced a renewal of thought and letters in the ninth century. During this time we find a concerted effort of appropriation and assimilation of literary sources, humanist and patristic, the outcome of which can be evaluated in the set of theological and political conceptions that became normative for Christian thought during these centuries.

Introduction to the English Translation

The Carolingian Renaissance lasted from the final quarter of the eighth century to the first quarter of the tenth. It comprised four distinct literary generations, the third of which covers the period which interests us, that of Charles the Bald, who died in 877. This youngest son of Louis the Pious (who died in 840) became king of the western part of France, according to the treaty of Verdun. He displayed and executed superior military and diplomatic skill in protecting his kingdom against invasions from his own brothers from the east as well as incursions of Vikings from the west. Alongside these efforts, his lack of familial ties with the populace of his kingdom made him that much more attentive to encouraging literary activity on the part of his subjects and his clergy. Following the example of his grandfather Charlemagne, who availed himself of the spiritual and cultural assistance of Alcuin, Charles exercised care and discernment in selecting persons who could help him achieve his goals: Walafrid Strabo, the first director of his school; Archbishop Hincmar of Rheims, whose personality as well as doctrinal and theological position we shall discover later; Lupus of Ferrières, and others as well. Since he was able to act only with the support of the nobles and the church, Charles was very liberal in his treatment of the ecclesiastical community, making grants to monasteries as well as distributing monetary, financial, and commercial privileges to the church. He was himself interested, all the while, in mathematics and theology. Poems which were dedicated to him recognized him as much for his liberality as for his interest in studies. Among others, Eriugena, in his poem beginning with the words *Auribus aebraicis*, implores Christ to come to Charles's assistance against the barbarians and praises the king as patron of the church.[5]

The most salient fact for our consideration is the partisan and effective participation of King Charles in the theological disputes of his time. In that regard, he had been formed by the teaching and especially the spirit of his tutor, Lupus of Ferrières. Faithful to Alcuin, Lupus considered intellectual formation to be a journey whose goal was the study of the Bible and the truths of faith. He could have subscribed to what Alcuin wrote at the outset of his *Grammar:* "My dear children: may your youth develop each day along the path of the arts in such a way that an age more mature and a mind more robust will be able to attain the heights of the Holy Scriptures. In that way, fully armed, you will become invincible defenders

---

5. See also D. Moran, *The Philosophy of John Scotus Erigena* (Cambridge, 1989), 17.

and preachers of the true faith."[6] Reading and explication of the Scriptures were indeed the principal tasks one might accomplish in entrusting oneself to the teaching of the Fathers: mostly the Latin Fathers and those among the Greek Fathers cited by the Latins, excerpted in the canonical collections, or for whom traditional translations were extant.

We know the sources available in the private library of Charles the Bald, a library for his own use and probably not accessible to the Palatine School. Among other works it contained *The Life of Charlemagne* by Einhard, the treatise *De tribus quaestionibus* of Lupus of Ferrières, one by Hincmar on the soul, treatises on the Eucharist by Ratramnus of Corbie and Paschasius Radbertus, as well as the works of Augustine. The library of Wulfad, the friend of Eriugena to whom he dedicated the *Periphyseon* and abbot of Saint Médard at Soissons and later bishop of Bourges, was even more ample, including works by Bede, Isidore, Ambrose, and Augustine. To be sure, all these sources could not be said to be known with equal precision; those who cited them often did so at second or third hand. Moreover, no one employed a historical-critical method to decipher them, which could have cast light on the diverse and sometimes contradictory stages in the intellectual evolution of their authors. This is especially significant for reading the works of Augustine, where selected texts could just as well serve to justify *gemina praedestinatio:* the double predestination to punishment and to reward so dear to Gottschalk— indeed, he had braved two synods defending it—as the conviction, as Eriugena understood it, that human freedom of choice is the very heart of freedom.

Charles the Bald not only gave evidence of great interest in the theological controversies of his time, as we have noted, but even animated a few of them. A list of them can be found, albeit lacking relevant dates, which are far from easy to establish, in the treatise *De praedestinatione* composed by Hincmar of Rheims in 859–60.[7] What is striking about the debates, as well as a measure of what one may call the humanism of the Carolingian Renaissance, is the linkage uniting theology, psychology, and anthropology for the intellectuals of this period. This is especially clear when it comes to the problems posed by the theory of double predestination, as it leaves no room for human freedom. But it is also true of the

---

6. Alcuin, "Grammatica," *PL* 125.296D.
7. Hincmar, "De praedestinatione," *PL* 125.296D.

debate on the beatific vision, a question inextricably linked to problems articulating the relation of soul to body, and to the status of our natural capacities. That is why we must briefly call to mind the content and progress of these other two debates before focusing our attention on the controversy over predestination, since they display the same oppositions between the contrary positions. This comparison will allow us to better comprehend the reactions which Gottschalk's theology elicited, and especially the urgency with which Hincmar was impelled to have recourse to the judgment of Scottus Eriugena.

King Charles was particularly interested in the question of the relationship between soul and body. He had already asked Ratramnus of Corbie to delineate the teaching of different authors on the question of knowing whether the soul is circumscribed in place. Ratramnus had explained that, on account of the intellect, the soul transcended the limits of body. Charles the Bald then turned to Hincmar, who held a contrary position, namely that our souls are contained within our bodies. To justify his opinion, Hincmar appended to his response a florilegium of texts entitled "Quod anima sit in corpore."[8] He used this to counteract a position whose extreme consequence came in asserting a separation between our localized actions and our intellectual intentions, or so it seemed to him. We should note that both John the Scot and Gottschalk kept their distance from this discussion, yet the ideas at work in it were nonetheless present in their debate, however indirectly. Thus, in his pastoral letter "To the Simple Believers in His Diocese," which mentioned the errors of Gottschalk, Hincmar recounted that since 849, in his discussions of the vision of God, the monk "was more concerned with the way in which one might see him than with the merit which the vision assumes."[9] We know the position of Gottschalk from a letter which he wrote to Ratramnus of Corbie on the subject. There he indicates his desire to open a consultation regarding a passage of Saint Augustine's *De civitate Dei*, where the bishop of Hippo raises the possibility that either "God will be visible to our bodily eyes"—a supposition difficult or even impossible to justify from Scripture, or that "God will be known and visible in that He will

---

8. *PL* 125.948A–52D.
9. Hincmar, "Ad simplices" edited by W. Gundlach in "Zwei Schriften des Erzbischofs Hinkmar von Reims," *Zeitschrift für Kirchengeschichte* 10 (1889): 258–309.

Introduction to the English Translation

appear spiritually to each one of us," a position easier to comprehend.[10] Gottschalk had opted, despite Augustine's reservations, for a radical spiritualization of resurrected bodies. Lupus of Ferrières, one of Gottschalk's correspondents, laid out what could appear dangerous in his position: "The elucidations which I have just given . . . should make you understand, above all, that God will not be visible in any body, either properly or figuratively, to eyes which do not participate in intelligence: such a privilege is reserved to spirit alone."[11] The position which Gottschalk was defending resulted in radically severing any organic connection between intentions, choice, and human actions on the one side, and the ultimate reward of the beatific vision on the other. For that vision was no longer an accomplishment which succeeded in crowning the intellectual and voluntary efforts of the blessed, but a decree of God most high which changed the condition of corporeal matter. We shall note this fundamental tendency in the thought of Gottschalk again in the controversy over predestination. This was certainly the most animated debate of the ninth century and the only one in which John the Scot participated, so far as we know.

The Controversy over Predestination

It is crucial for understanding the thesis of double predestination, as Gottschalk defended it, to realize how intimately it is tied to his conception of time. The history of philosophy, as well as our own spiritual experience, shows us that there are two ways of perceiving and defining time, two intuitions which are given expression in two opposing images: the arrow which moves forward versus the indefinitely recurring cycle. The perception of time as an arrow is a principle of explication which puts the nonreversibility of history into relief, the unique and unforeseen character of each event, thereby underscoring the possibility of progress. The perception of time as a cycle considers history as a harmony planned out in advance. On this view of things, contingency in nature as well as the feeling harbored deep in the human heart according to which one might have done otherwise or might do better tomorrow, are utter illu-

---

10. Augustine, "De civitate Dei," XXII.29 (*PL* 41.800-801); Gottschalk, "Carmen ad Ratramnum, " *PL* 121.367-72.
11. Lupus of Ferrières, "Epistola ad Godescalcum," *PL* 119.491-92 (ed. E. Dümmler, 38).

sions. The outcome of human history is as implacable as the revolution of the planets.

It was the second of these two intuitions which struck Gottschalk, and which he succeeded in reducing into his extreme interpretation. For him, the circle of time contracts into a point, into the very instant in which God most high decrees the end of the history of each of His creatures. From that point on our acts lose all relevance; everything has been determined, "fixed," one might say, from the beginning. In one way, we might say that this vision finds its source in fascination with the perfection of God. In effect, what relevance could history have, with its run of contingencies, of successes and failures, in the face of the program of the Most High, a program foreseen from the beginning and one which He accomplishes in the details which He has fixed from eternity?

What characterized history conceived according to the arrow of time, namely the possibility of improvement or of deterioration, emerged in this vision as contrary to the perfection of God. In effect, if men could improve themselves with time, they would not have been created perfect; if they could deteriorate, that would mean that the program would not unfold according to a perfect law. What fascinated Gottschalk was the fullness of divine wisdom, from which he concluded that we must find therein the necessary strength to undertake what we will necessarily become, according to the divine plan: bodies either glorified or damned. Pastors and teachers of the faith could not help but be disturbed by so drastic a theological thesis, particularly one which concerned a question as fundamental as that of the connection between human freedom and our final beatitude. Hrabanus Maurus expressed his misgivings in a letter to Hincmar of Rheims in 848, requesting that he restrict Gottschalk to his diocese: "May your lordship know that an itinerant monk, who says that he is incardinated in your diocese, has arrived among us in Italy, and is spreading a pernicious doctrine of divine predestination, leading people into error. He supposes that the predestination of God extends to evil as well as good, and that there are men in this world who cannot correct their erroneous ways nor turn from sin, because the predestination of God impels them to [everlasting] death."[12]

The scrutiny to which ecclesiastical and teaching authorities submitted this thesis elicited a long and sharp controversy. We should not be

---

12. Hrabanus Maurus, "Epistola synodialis," *PL* 112.1574-76.

Introduction to the English Translation

surprised to find King Charles the Bald directly interested in this debate, exercising his authority in selecting theologians whose opinion he solicited, or in convoking councils where these theological questions would be debated. Gottschalk had in effect disseminated a doctrine which threatened to undermine the authentic Christian humanism of the Carolingian kingdom by upsetting the delicate balance between divine wisdom and the possibility for men to follow the path of justice. The authority to which all sides had recourse during the debate was clearly that of Saint Augustine. But Gottschalk compromised the goal and the program which Augustine had proposed in the *City of God*. Let us recall briefly the general structure of this great work, as Augustine himself conveyed it to his friend Firmus, the publicist. He made clear in his letter that we are faced with a composition in two distinct parts: one part refuting the vanities of the impious, the other clarifying our religion. From the initial pages, in effect, the *City of God* was directed not only to Christians exercising their desire to deepen their faith, but also to unbelievers curious to know something about this religion. At the end of his exposition, Augustine directed himself to his pagan interlocutor and challenged him one last time to make the "passage to the city of God" by acknowledging the universal mediation of the man-God, Jesus Christ. As for Christians, they must prepare themselves for eternal beatitude which will be theirs after the judgment, by entrusting themselves to the divine promises. The vision of God, adapted to the capacities of each, yet fully satisfying the hopes and capacities of all, must be their only goal, giving direction to their earthly existence: "for what other aim could be ours but to arrive at the kingdom which has no end?"[13]

In this way Saint Augustine had succeeded in holding together the two perceptions of time which we have just opposed. History is governed by the immutable wisdom of God, but it has a direction and admits of improvement. The goal of history, restoring all things in Christ, will comprise the time of a yet more exalted state than that of the first creation. Contemplating all the images and traces of Himself which God has left in creation, even after the fall, anchors our experience in a state which transcends infinitely anything we could imagine.[14] The doctor of Hippo succeeded in this way to ground the delicate balance between the om-

---

13. "De civitate Dei," 22.309.5 (*PL* 41.804G).
14. "De civitate Dei," 22.12.24.

nipotence of God's wisdom and the hope inscribed in human freedom. This was the very thesis which threatened the theory of Gottschalk. Hincmar, who with Hrabanus Maurus had negotiated at this time the reconciliation of Charles the Bald with the emperor Lothar, asked counsel as to how to proceed while Gottschalk waited at Orbais. A synod of bishops was to take place at the royal residence of Quierzy in February–March 849. Hincmar arraigned the condemned man in the presence of King Charles. He was condemned again, and the sentence read: "We decree, by our episcopal authority, that you shall be flogged and confined, according to the regulations, to prison. And lest you continue to presume to teach your doctrines, we impose an eternal silence on your mouth, by virtue of the eternal Word."[15] Hincmar had chosen as his place of confinement the monastery of Hautvillers which was within his own jurisdiction.

Nevertheless, Gottschalk managed to continue his theological reflection and propagate his thesis. This is the point where he proposed the consultation regarding the beatific vision, to which we have already alluded. Hincmar, fearing that the heresy was spreading, composed a long pastoral letter entitled "To Simple Believers," addressed to the faithful of his diocese. As we shall see, the wording was not very propitious, for it left the impression that Hincmar had put water in the wine of pure doctrine, either from weakness or from following an exaggerated concern not to ask too much from the weak and the childlike. Moreover, once having decided, with Pardulus of Laon, to solicit opinions from many theologians, Hincmar discovered that he was doctrinally quite alone. The first of the masters consulted, Prudentius of Troyes, responded that predestination to death and to life was in fact a cardinal principle of true doctrine. Ratramnus of Corbie attacked Hincmar's pastoral letter in a communication addressed to Gottschalk himself.[16] Hrabanus Maurus, tired and aging, confined himself to concurring with the opposition to Hincmar, and stated that he would henceforth decline to participate in debate. Finally, Lupus de Ferrières was solicited by King Charles himself to write a treatise, *De tribus quaestionibus*,[17] in which he joined in with the position of the other theologians, criticizing the pastoral letter "To Simple Believers."

---

15. Hincmar, "Ad simplices" (ed. W. Gundlach, 308–9).
16. Hrabanus Maurus, "Epistola ad Hincmarum," *PL* 119.621–46.
17. Lupus of Ferrières, "De tribus quaestionibus," *PL* 119.621–48.

Introduction to the English Translation

Hincmar received these documents from Charles the Bald himself, so one can imagine his consternation. He had, he believed, the right to expect support from such a theologian in defending the thesis which allowed one to uphold the omnipotence of God together with the fullness of God's knowledge, on the one hand, and the unique character of the human creature, *capax boni et mali*, on the other. How could it diminish the perfection of God if one saw God as creator of human beings endowed with reason and will, and so be able to meet the questions which life poses them in a creative fashion? Taking counsel from Pardulus, Hincmar decided to solicit the help of a master of the palatine court hitherto removed from the debate: one whose knowledge and authority was all the more esteemed in that he enjoyed the favor of the king, the learned John the Scot.

The Text

The *De praedestinatione* of Eriugena comes to us in one manuscript only, originating from Corbie. It consists of a preface, nineteen chapters and an epilogue.[18] The nineteen summaries which he himself placed at the head of each chapter give an adequate idea of its structure and content. The work is abundantly documented: besides numerous texts from Scripture, Scottus Eriugena cites Augustine as his principal source, Gregory the Great, Isidore, and among pagan authors, Cicero, as well as Boethius, and closer to hand, Alcuin. Nonetheless, this veritable arsenal of Carolingian culture was made to serve and support a thesis which appeared quite revolutionary. Scottus Eriugena appealed to the tribunal of reason to show that it condemned, along with the entire tradition judiciously interpreted, any idea of predestination. His thesis is clear, radical, and straightforward: Gottschalk was wrong; no one can hold double predestination. Given that God is eternal, we cannot say that He foresees or predetermines. Beyond that, to think that God foresees sin and punishment is silly: evil does not exist, being a pure absence, so one cannot know it. To think that God has prepared hell from the beginning of time for human beings is a pitiful anthropomorphism. God is the Good above all goods and the source of all good. The only punishment is immanent to sin itself, confining sinners in the prison of their own conscience.

---

18. *PL* 122.355–440.

Introduction to the English Translation

Scottus Eriugena bases his reasoning here on the young Augustine, disciple of Plotinus, and especially on his treatise *De vera religione*. In doing so he managed to propose a vision of human beings which could hardly satisfy Hincmar: a vital and dynamic correlation between will, memory, and knowledge. The concept of freedom is constitutive of human willing. God could not, at the price of contradiction, will human beings to be what they are, while at the same time removing their freedom. Of the two images of time—arrow or cycle—which we have contrasted, Eriugena opts for the arrow: in their very essence, human beings have this possibility to resist whatever limits their intellectual inquiry or restricts their will. After the redaction of *De praedestinatione*, the theologians engaged in the controversy surrounding Gottschalk found themselves facing two diametrically opposed visions of the relationship between man and God, inspired by two contrary conceptions of history: one for which progress was only apparent, as in Gottschalk; the other according to which progress was the very law of history. As for the reality of time, there is either the creating "now" in which all has been decreed, for Gottschalk, or a pure élan giving each instant a novelty which escapes any foreseeing, for Scottus.

It is hardly surprising that the *De praedestinatione* was a scandal and succeeded in arraying against Scottus Eriugena all the argumentation of those defending Gottschalk, while compromising the adversaries of the monk, who had opposed Gottschalk as champions of orthodoxy yet were now suspected of sharing and favoring the errors of Scottus. Hincmar regretted having solicited his collaboration: such a protagonist was most dangerous to those whose cause he proposed to serve! The other side published vigorous refutations. Wenilo, archbishop of Sens, selected parts of each chapter and sent them to Prudentius of Troyes, who composed a substantial work on predestination: *De praedestinatione contra Joannem Scotum*, published in 852 with a preface by Wenilon.[19] It is a compact discussion, taking chapter by chapter as a dialectician would. Although Prudentius knew Scottus, he treated him harshly, accusing him of having revived the heresies of Pelagianism and of Origen and of being another Julian of Eclanum. He had recourse to an irony which, with regard to Eriugena's display of learning, could only be called biting.

---

19. Prudentius of Troyes, "De praedestinatione contra Joannem Scotum, " *PL* 115. 1109–1366.

Introduction to the English Translation

Scottus had given his detractors a field day: seventy-seven propositions taken from his book were refuted in this manner. As a final blow, a group which could boast of the best names of theology in the kingdom of Charles the Bald—Ratramnus, Lupus of Ferrières, and Prudentius—mobilized to defend the authentic Augustinianism which they felt to be threatened by the condemnation of Gottschalk. Deemed responsible, however indirectly, for the book of John the Scot, Hincmar was forced to defend his prestige and authority. Having received from Charles the Bald the dossier compiled against Scottus, and against his specific *capitula*, Hincmar responded by way of an immense work (presently lost), in which he confirmed his hostility to the thesis of Gottschalk while awkwardly repudiating the *pultes scotticae*. But this was hardly enough to calm the waters. For the theologians of Lyons and of Sens, Hincmar would always be the enemy of augustinianism and the ally of Eriugena. So he composed a new volume of modest proportions, *De praedestinatione*, and dedicated it (as he had the earlier one) to Charles the Bald. But the defenders of double predestination did not lay down their arms but rather worked to win the favor of Pope Nicholas I. According to Prudentius, the Pope confirmed the doctrine of double predestination and that of redemption "for all believers" before the end of 859. This pontifical stance was doubtless the cause of Hincmar's loss of heart, as he ceased to pursue the debate. He no longer sought to impose his theology, looking rather for ways to end the battle and save his honor. He composed a synodal letter which we still possess, a masterpiece of political conciliation, whose formulae are sufficiently vague to be adopted by all the protagonists in the debate as well as the faithful at large, while carefully disguising what was at issue in the debate. He treated Christian dogmas and attacks on church property in one breath, elucidating in no particular order the doctrine of God, the Trinity, angels, human beings, the fall, redemption, and the sacraments. He included a sentence which could please everyone without compromising the truth: "*qui vult omnes homines salvos fieri . . . quique corporis morte in cruce pro omnibus debitoribus . . . omnes qui salvandi sunt, id est omnes praedestinati.*"[20] In this way peace was restored and each party could retain its positions. Prudentius of Troyes and Florus of Lyons were

---

20. Hincmar, "Epistola concilii Tusiacensis ad rerum ecclesiaticarum pervasores et ad pauperum praedatores," *PL* 126.123C, 124D, 126B; see also "De praedestinatione," *PL* 125.55–474.

free to interpret *omnes* and *omnibus* in a restricted sense, and *vult* in the sense of a decree fixed once and for all.

Of all those involved, Gottschalk alone profited nothing from the armistice, whose tepid outcome could hardly satisfy him. He tried his luck again in turning to Pope Nicholas I and in soliciting a response from the council of Metz (863). Hincmar absented himself from the council, and the pope died in 867. Deprived of communion and ecclesiastical burial, the itinerant monk died soon after. As for John the Scot, the incident of his intervention had no further unpleasant consequences for him, beyond the sharp and ironic replies of Prudentius and Florus, and the criticisms of the councils of Valence and Langres. We have already seen how Hincmar, aware of his misstep, had little by little disassociated his theology from the master to whom he had appealed. He did his best to suppress the entire affair. The only time he ever again mentioned the name of John the Scot was to deny any connection to his own part in the debate. Perhaps he hoped to drown his own zeal in forgetfulness.

In fact, however, the debate continued from one council to another, and from synod to synod, until the end of the century. Indeed, has it ever ceased in the history of Christian theology or in the inner experience of Christian holiness? The benefit—if the word applies and benefit there be—of the Gottschalk affair is to have clearly shown that the Carolingian Renaissance had hardly achieved unanimity regarding these questions touching the personal life of the faithful as much as the cultural balance of the City of God. The extended controversy of the ninth century featuring Gottschalk proved but one episode in the everlasting struggle between two tendencies which divided the human spirit; indeed one might add, between two ways of appealing to the theology of Augustine. For some, like Ratramnus, Lupus of Ferrières, Remigius, or Florus, who had recourse to the writings of his anti-Pelagian period, it was always a matter of affirming unequivocally the primacy of the divine will. For others, like Hrabanus Maurus or Hincmar, who based their ideas on the writings of the period when Augustine was combating the Manichees, the issue was safeguarding the goodness of God and the free interplay of human action in the drama of salvation. What is certain is that Scottus Eriugena could not but feel alien to that division of minds. What is more, as much because of his culture and his dialectical skill as well as the originality of his insights, he was unable not to appear a stranger to the discussion, even to those who had recourse to him. Men of power and of action, like Hincmar and Hrabanus Maurus, would have preferred to understand predestination as a foreknowledge of the merits of good works, while keeping God in the role of a simple witness to the struggle for which he crowned the victors.

It is clear that John the Scot had no further role in the debate. Removed from the controversy, he continued to enjoy the protection of Charles the Bald, developing in his *Periphyseon* the metaphysics of the return to God which undergirded his thesis. In this work, he elucidates the relation between God and the world, so explicating all that is required of human beings who adopt this vision of the world. It is, in a word, courage: "the courage, above all, to engage in philosophy, that is, to pose the question of being and nonbeing. The courage to continue the never-ending task of breaking every idol, exposing every false identification, to return to the place of one's true identity, the 'nonbeing' *par excellence,* to live in an 'unknowing' analogous to the 'unknowing' of God."[21] For John the Scot, human freedom and beatitude come only at this price.

Translated by David Burrell and Edward D. English

---

21. Wohlman, *L'homme, le monde sensible et le péché,* 606.

Treatise on Divine Predestination

Preface

To the most illustrious lords Hincmar and Pardulus worthy and pre-eminent guardians of the christian faith and endowed from above by the father of lights with the divine gift of episcopal grace, John your devoted servant offers greetings in the Lord.

I cannot express the quantity or the quality of the thanks I owe you for having deigned in your generous and great affection to choose me as your collaborator as one having some ability to defend the salvation of us all, namely the catholic faith. Although far from possessing the competence of your powers in words and understanding, yet I trust that through faith and dedication I am capable of proclaiming the truth. Your attention is partly drawn upwards in contemplation towards the exploration of the truth and partly faced downwards in the activity of governing the church. We, on the other hand, tossed around, as it were, like some small boat with waves on many sides, in the midst of the surging sail-winged sea of the rule of our master, namely the glorious lord Charles, even when stabilised in the haven of his fair weather are scarcely ever allowed even the shortest interval of time to scan the records of wisdom. Nevertheless in the measure of our ability, such as it may be, we will give testimony to your prudent and sound doctrine. For, just as the greatest and brightest lights of the world do not despise the nightly shining of the stars but make use of their rays to perfect their own brilliance so as to drive away all the gloom of darkness, so you, most reverend fathers, although the renown of your eloquence is sufficient to guard against, to overcome, and to destroy all the subtlety of newly hatched heresies, yet you have not scorned to strengthen your perfect definition of the faith of predestination by the affirmation of our reasoning, so that the noble vigour of your piety may be evident to all and the not despicable lowliness of our obedience may be manifest.

In this work of ours, therefore, which we have taken pains to write at your command in testimony to your orthodox faith, what you perceive as true hold on to and attribute to the catholic church; what is false reject and pardon us as being human; what is doubtful believe until authority decrees that it is to be rejected, or is true or is always to be believed. But as to inelegance of the style, I do not think that the steadfastness of your mind should be so easily disturbed that weariness of listening should take hold of your ears before the desire to reach the conclusions I have worked so hard at advocating. If these are true, truth is to be esteemed in them regardless of verbal considerations. Indeed, as Augustine says,[1] it is an outstanding characteristic of virtuous minds to love the truth in words, not the words themselves. For what is the use of a golden key if it cannot open what we want, or what objection is there to a wooden one if it can do this, when all we seek is that what is closed be opened. Accept freely then these small tokens of our talent, which are rather to be reflected upon for their usefulness, if any, than to be examined for the grace of their style which is little or non-existent.

Finally we humbly entreat your clemency that whenever you find that we have spoken of the equality of divine foreknowledge and predestination you will understand that we have intended the unity of the divine substance in which they are one. Also our statement that the things that are not can neither be known nor foreknown by God, you should not

---

1. *De doctrina christiana* IV, 11, 26 (*Christian Instruction* E 9; NPN 2; FC 2; CUA 23). There will be frequent reference to the works of St. Augustine. English translations of these works are to be found in the following series: *The Works of Aurelius Augustinus*, Edinburgh (E); *Ancient Christian Writers* (ACW); *Library of Christian Classics* (CC); Catholic University of America, Patristic Studies (CUA); *Fathers of the Church* (FC); *A Select Library of Nicene and Post-Nicene Fathers* (NPN). There will also be an occasional reference to Migne *Patrologiae latine cursus completus* (PL).

Preface

regard as having been made out of that perverseness with which some people try to deny the foreknowledge of God, but out of that reasoning by means of which we are taught that the things that are not are not known and that the knowledge of God is his substance, but his substance exists not in nothing but in something.

> May the peace of Christ overflow in your hearts.
> Under the rule of Charles the glory of the Franks abounds.
> As the seas with fish, near shore and in the deep:
> The sect of devilish doctrine is condemned
> And under shepherds' care faith shines in loveliness.

CHAPTER ONE

That Every Question Is Solved by the Fourfold System of the Four Rules of the Whole of Philosophy[2]

1. Every true and complete doctrinal system by which the theory of all things is most assiduously inquired into and most clearly ascertained is established within that discipline which the Greeks usually call *philosophia*. We have, therefore, considered it necessary to discuss briefly its divisions or constituent parts. If, indeed, as Saint Augustine says, it is believed and taught as the fundamental principle of man's salvation that philosophy, that is the study of wisdom, is not one thing and religion another—for they whose teaching we do not favour do not in fact participate with us in the sacraments[3]—what else is the exercise of philosophy but the exposition of the rules of true religion by which the supreme and principal cause of all things, God, is worshipped with humility and rationally searched for? It follows then that true philosophy is true religion and conversely that true religion is true philosophy. While philosophy

---

2. This chapter title was supplied by the text's editors from quotations from Prudentius of Troyes and Florus of Lyon. Titles of other chapters form part of Eriugena's text.
3. *De uera religione* 5, 8 (*True Religion* CC 6) and cf. *ibid.* 1, 1.

may in many and various ways be divided up, it is seen, however, to have twice two principal parts necessary for the solution of every question. These the Greeks have been pleased to name ΔΙΑΙΡΕΤΙΚΗ, ΟΡΙСΤΙΚΗ, ΑΠΟΔΙΚΤΙΚΗ, ΑΝΑΛΙΤΙΚΗ, and in Latin we can call these *diuisoria* (divisory), *diffinitiua* (defining), *demonstratiua* (demonstrative), and *resolutiua* (resolutionary). Of these, the first by dividing one into many, separates; the second, by determining one from among many, concludes; the third, by indicating what is hidden through what is manifest, reveals; the fourth, by separating compound into simple, resolves.

2. We shall also show examples of those in the course of this work, to the extent that the light itself which illuminates the heart of its seekers will have opened our approach to the matters we are trying to enter into. No man instructed in the art of disputation has any doubt that it is indeed by means of those four parts, as by some useful and honourable fourfold method[4] of human reasoning, that the very art of disputation, which is truth, is arrived at. The rules of that art are indispensably prescribed for us once we are compelled to reply to a certain lover-of-the-putrid called Gottschalk, author as well as advocate of his own heresy, together with his supporters—though I do not know if there are any, and wish that there were not! And we are constrained to reply specifically on the instructions of the vigilant pastors of the catholic church within whose sheepfold such poison is striving to creep. We have, too, the particular approval of the most orthodox prince and venerable lord, Charles, whose greatest concern is to harbour devout and proper sentiments towards God, to refute the distorted teachings of heretics by true reasonings and the authority of the holy Fathers, and to root them out utterly to the last one.

3. Therefore, lest we defenders of the truth appear to contend without weapons with the advocates of falsehood, it will be appropriate for us to observe the rules of the art of disputation. For, since, through the art of rhetoric both the true and the false are urged,[5] who would dare to say that in its defenders truth must stand unarmed against falsehood? The result, of course, would be that those who try to promote false information would know how by their introduction to make the listener well-disposed

---

4. *Quadriuium* : Madec in a note to his edition observes that Eriugena adapts to dialectic the term applied by Boethius (*Institutio arithmetica* I, 1) to mathematical sciences.

5. Cf. Augustine, *De doct. christ.* IV, 2, 3.

Fourfold System of the Four Rules

or attentive or amenable and the other would not know. The former set forth the false briefly, clearly and with the veneer of truth; the others set forth the truth in such a way that they are tedious to listen to, not clearly understandable and in the end not willingly believed. The former oppose the truth by fallacious argument and assert falsehood; the others are powerless to defend the truth or refute falsehood. The former, stirring and urging the minds of their audience to error, by their eloquence terrify, sadden, cheer and passionately exhort them; while the others, for the sake of truth, slowly and feebly allow the attention to flag. Who can be so foolish as to think this wise? But since it is most truly written: "Many heresies must occur in order that the excellent among you may be recognised,"[6] let us also take advantage of this favour of divine providence. For heretics arise from among the kind of men who, even if they were in the church, would nevertheless wander from the truth. When, however, they are outside it, they are of great use, not for teaching the truth, of which they are ignorant, but by exciting worldly men to seek the truth and unworldly catholics to unveil the truth. There are, indeed, in the holy church innumerable men acceptable to God; but these men do not become manifest among us for as long as we are complacent about the darkness of our ignorance and prefer to lie asleep rather than look upon the light of truth. For that reason it is through heretics that many people are roused from sleep to look upon God's daylight and rejoice. Therefore let us make use even of heretics, not so as to approve of their errors but to be more watchful and wary in affirming catholic doctrine against their wiles even if we are unable to draw them back to salvation.

4. Therefore, since the unhappiness of the ancient enemy forever makes him envious of human happiness, he never ceases to devise plots against our salvation. Our salvation, on the other hand, takes its beginning from faith; he strives, therefore, to destroy faith, seeking out suitable vessels by which from outside into the ears of believers who are powerless to guard against the force of his cunning he may pour those poisons which his argumentative wickedness inwardly contrives. But because all the fresh devices which he has used until recently in striving to split the unity of the catholic faith have been utterly discredited by the workings of divine grace through those who have walked holy and unblemished in the

---

6. 1 Cor. 11.19; for the remainder of the passage cf. Augustine, *De uera relig.* 8, 15.

way of the law of the Lord, and have sought out his testimonies, now, lest he should neglect any subject for his wicked argument, he is attempting by a new stratagem to breach the defences of a secure faith. For through his servant, namely Gottschalk,[7] he maintains that there are in God two predestinations, and thereby he tries to deny the most equitable rewards of justice and the most merciful gifts of grace. For, since the human race is divided into the good and the bad—and, as truth states, the end of the bad is eternal punishment but of the good eternal life—who are the bad but the godless, and who the good but the just? The unavoidable and operative cause of all the just is, as he affirms, established in one predestination; similarly the cause of the wicked in the other. For one predestination, as he says, is of the just, the other of the wicked, so much so that no one, except by the immutable necessity of the one predestination, can either attain to his just reward or to his highest end, that is eternal life, nor anyone, except by an equal necessity of the other, be compelled to sink into the punishment his wickedness merits, or into the eternal torment which is its end.

This foolish and merciless lunacy is in the first place refuted by divine authority; secondly it is annulled by the rules of right reason. Why! Is it not said by the prophet: "all the ways of the Lord are mercy and truth"?[8] This is explained more clearly elsewhere: "I shall sing to your mercy and justice, O Lord."[9] In those words the generosity of God's gifts and the equity of his justice are most clearly commended.

---

7. C. Lambot, ed., *Oeuvres théologiques et grammaticales de Godescalc d'Orbais*, p. 14, 5-19.
8. Ps. 24.10.
9. Ps. 100.1.

CHAPTER TWO

From the Argument of Necessity It Is Concluded That There Cannot Be Two Predestinations

1. Where then, Gottschalk, are the inevitabilities of your two predestinations? I say yours, not God's; for it was your perversity that invented them and for that reason they do not and cannot exist. How indeed could that exist which attempts to do away with that which does exist? Moreover where there is inevitability there is no will. In God, however, there is will. In him, therefore, there is no necessity. God made all that he made of his own will and out of no necessity. For what could compel God to create anything?[10] But if some cause did compel him to create, we would be right in believing that it is greater and better than he. And for that reason it, and not he, would be worshipped as the supreme cause of all things and as God. But if we devoutly believe and correctly understand that the one and chief cause of the entire universe is the will of God, it is vain to imagine that necessity is either in that will or prior to it. Come now: if all that is in God is God, and if the will of God is in God, the will

---

10. Cf. Augustine, *De diuersis quaestionibus 83*, qu. 28 (*Eighty-three Different Questions* FC 70) and cf. id., *De Genesi contra Manichaeos* 1, 2, 4, (PL XXXIV, 175).

of God is, therefore, God. For him there is no distinction between being and willing; rather for him being is identical with willing. Accordingly, if the will of God is free—and to believe otherwise is wicked—and if the free will is devoid of all necessity, then no necessity has hold of the will of God. And, of course, whatever we understand concerning the divine will we must necessarily understand in the same way of his predestination also. But all necessity is excluded from the divine will. Therefore it is excluded from his predestination.

2. But perhaps you say, you heretic, that his will but not his predestination belongs to the substance of God in such a way that for God, while there is no difference between being and willing, there is a difference between being and predestining? But we can easily refute that by an argument which is taken from the definition of predestination. For divine predestination is, as Augustine says, the preparation and arrangement before time began of all that God is going to do. If, then, we believe and understand that before time began nothing existed except God alone—but that God's predestination existed before all creation no sane person disputes—the inference is that God's predestination is God himself and belongs to his nature. But perhaps you may say: what is said of God before the world was made is by no means always said according to his substance: for some things are stated substantially, but others indeed relatively: for instance, he is called father, son, lord, not according to substance but according to relation; similarly his predestination is proposed in relation to those things that are predestined. Listen to the passage of Scripture[11] saying of Christ: "In whom are hidden away all the treasures of knowledge and wisdom." Tell me, I ask, what are you trying to understand from these words? Do you perhaps judge the knowledge and wisdom of Christ to be accidents but not according to his own divine substance? It is absurd to believe this and false to advocate it. For he is the highest intellect in which all things exist together—rather he is himself all things although called by a variety of names which take their meaning from the rational nature which was created in order to search him out. He, however, is in himself one and the same, being the simple and multiple cause of all natures.[12] For God, then, being is wisdom, wisdom is knowing, and knowing is choosing.

---

11. Col. 2.3.
12. Cf. Augustine, *De trinitate* VI, 4, 6; 6, 8; 7, 8 *et passim* (*The Trinity* E7; CC 8; FC 45; NPN 3).

There Cannot Be Two Predestinations

For although all predestination is called foreknowledge but not all foreknowledge is called predestination, nevertheless we do not say that all predestination is foreknowledge and that not all foreknowledge is predestination in the same way as we are accustomed to speak of the *genera* and their forms. For example, in the virtues with which the rational soul is adorned *all* prudence is virtue but *not every* virtue is prudence; but, as we do rightly say, that which is virtue is prudence and that which is prudence is virtue. For in this way we do not signify virtue in general and its form, but we express only the unity of the nature of virtue and prudence. Therefore all predestination is rightly said to be foreknowledge, but not all foreknowledge predestination, so that we would understand that to foreknow is to predestine and to predestine is to foreknow; for they are of one and the same, that is divine, substance and nature. Yet not all of what we understand when we hear of God's foreknowledge must be understood by us when we hear of predestination: just as not all of what we look for in the word virtue do we necessarily look for in the word prudence. But it would be appropriate here to elaborate a little on this line of argument, which is taken from effects to cause.

3. The virtues of the soul are really nothing other than the effects of the one great cause of all things itself, namely the divine will. They might, then, be understood in such a way that, although they are many, they are yet at the same time inseparably linked because they are of the same nature. For of those things of which a single cause is inferred, a common nature is deduced; where one true virtue is found, there all virtues are reasonably proved to be. Nevertheless they permit of designation by a variety of names and division into the *genera* and the forms of that one true virtue, down to its individual species followed by multiplication into numerical individuals.[13] For the virtues are said to be as many as those on whom they are bestowed. Why wonder, then, about the ineffable cause itself of things which, although it may be wanting in *genera*, forms and individual numbers, yet from it is every *genus*, every form, every whole, every individual, because it is itself the primary essence of the universe. In fact, from it everything that exists has its being; it is the highest form of all things. What but that form does every thing desire that desires the

---

13. *Numeros:* In a footnote (note 110, p. 234) to *Periphyseon* I, p. 102, I, 18 (*PL* 471A) Sheldon-Williams points out Eirugena's use of *numerus* within the same paragraph to indicate both the individual and "the abstract quality of numerousness."

beginning of all things, whether consciously or unconsciously? From it is every whole, for in itself it is forever a whole; from it is every individual, because in itself it is a multiple without limit, number without number. Although, then, this divine substance itself, or essence or nature or however it may be described, is in itself one, undivided and inseparable—for unity is simple and immutable—yet it is named by various verbal expressions according to the dispositions of the human mind by which that mind strives to return to the knowledge of its creator. For a person who has misused his own free judgment cannot without toil and effort and the gift of cooperating grace attain to that which he had effortlessly abandoned.

4. Hence human reason, guided by truth, understanding its God in a multiplicity of ways, names him according to the modes of its own understanding by various descriptive designations. To take just a few of the possible examples: whenever the insight of reason touches upon the eternal intelligence in which all things are, namely God himself, it perceives that there the divine intelligence itself possesses a very complete and perfect notion of its own eternal and immutable substance, going beyond the understanding of any creature. This divine notion by which God understands himself is properly called wisdom. But when that same reason is joined to eternal intelligence, so that in it reason sees an incomprehensible notion of all the natures that have been created by that intelligence, reason thereupon names it knowledge. Again this is called knowledge quasi-properly, as it is observed not only in all those good things which God disposed to be made from and in his whole creation, before they were made, but also in all evil things. Those occur when a rational creature, impelled in the wrong direction, misuses his free will, that is when he abandons his creator and rushes headlong into wanton passion for the lowest things, which nevertheless are of God's creation.

5. As has been said, then, that very divine and in some sense universal preconception of all God's good things and all the evils of a corrupt creation merits the name of foreknowledge. And on account of this God is said to foreknow the good and the bad, that is if evil can be foreknown, a mode of expression which will be explained in what follows. But that same knowledge, to make a distinction in specific meanings, is expressly called predestination only when it is perceived in the works of God. The work of God is, in fact, discerned not only in the creation of all creatures but also in those whom God, through the favourable purpose of his grace, has prepared for eternal life. It is also discerned in that most secret opera-

tion by which he rightly abandons the evil motions of the wicked and attends to the exercise of justice on behalf of those whom by his predestination he has called. It is also in the very qualities of the elements which, while by their nature they appear to be good because they derive from the highest good, nevertheless are experienced as punishment by those for whom, according to their just deserts, the just judge has prepared eternal torments. And thus they are said to be evil although they are by their nature good. Therefore by this chain of reasoning it is proved that predestination is in God according to substance but cannot be so relatively.

6. Hence if it is not inappropriate for us to designate the one immutable essence of God and his indivisible simplicity by the name of wisdom, the name of knowledge, and by other names such as virtue, power, justice, truth, eternity, activity, and the like, it necessarily follows that by the name of predestination there is also very appropriately suggested the nature of that same inseparable essence. Then if it is irreverent to teach that there are two essences in God, or two wisdoms, knowledges, virtues; and that all the other qualities attributed to God are doubled or trebled or heaped up in some kind of multiple fashion, anyone who is proved to have stated that there are two predestinations in God is involved in the charge of ungodliness. For there is one divine predestination, just as there is one divine operation, one divine wisdom, one divine substance, one divine will.

Say then, Gottschalk, where can one find those two predestinations which you affirm? True reason does not allow for their existence in God, for the most part because of the force of necessity which you maintain is within them. Scripture in fact proclaims: "Great are the works of the lord, discerned in all that he wills";[14] elsewhere: "whatsoever he has willed, all those things the lord has done."[15] It did not say: in all his necessities, but: in all that he wills, which is free of all necessity. Although indeed all things whatsoever that God has willed needs must come to be, nevertheless no necessity either forces his will to do anything or restrains it from doing anything. For who resists his will? But we say that all things whatsoever that God wills to take place must needs be, in the sense that we must understand that everything that God wills to take place must not be otherwise than as he willed. Indeed those things that he willed exist, and

14. Ps. 110.2
15. Ps. 113.3.

they exist because he willed them to be. And for this reason the necessity of the divine will strikes those who have the proper discernment as nothing other than that will itself. Therefore just as by the divine will those things arise which do arise, so by his will they arise not otherwise than according as that will has willed. For if the necessity of all natures is the will of God, the will of God will be the necessity of natures.[16] But the will of God is the necessity of the natures which it has itself created. Therefore the necessity of the natures which God has created will be the will of God. And anything we understand about the divine will we must doubtless also understand about God's predestination.

---

16. Cf. Augustine, *De Genesi ad litteram* VI, 15, 26 (*PL* XXXIV, 350).

CHAPTER THREE

Reason Does Not Permit of Two Predestinations

1. Now at this point let us briefly go back over all the conclusions of the arguments already set out. Firstly, then, true reason recommends that the divine will is the highest, principal and sole cause of all things the Father has made through his truth, and that that will itself is in every way free of all necessity which would either force it or hinder it, but is itself its own necessity; therefore it is wholly will. Secondly, in the way that that will is most correctly predicated of God according to substance, so most certainly is predestination predicated. This can be proved by the argument from wisdom and knowledge and truth, and by the other attributes which none of the faithful doubts are substantially predicated of God. In the same way, if all necessity is removed from the divine will, it will most certainly be removed from divine predestination. Indeed for God it is not one thing to will, another to predestine, since everything he has made he has willed by predestining and predestined by willing. Also the words by which the rational soul seeks to indicate its God signify one and the same thing, that is the ineffable essence itself of the creator, although some of the names may be used relatively. The motion of the human mind by which it returns to its beginning strives to ascend gradually, and thus,

according to the means of its ascent, it comes upon verbal symbols by which, in obedience to charity, it imparts its inner understanding to the senses of those who are ascending or desire to ascend with it.

Next it follows likewise that if all the things that are predicated of God are one, but nothing is more truly or more honourably predicated of God than predestination, it therefore is one; and this Gottschalk both erroneously divides up and blasphemously denies, and instead of it has thought up for himself two, of which neither one nor the other can stand up. By right, therefore, they are completely non-existent because they are neither true nor false. They are not true since everything that contradicts the truth is not from the truth.[17] Everything that is from the truth needs must be true; therefore everything that contradicts the truth must be untrue. But the two predestinations of Gottschalk contradict the truth. Therefore they are not true. They are not false. For everything false seeks under some guise of truth to be what it is not. An example of this in the nature of things is the reflected sound of a voice which by the Greeks is called *Echo* (HXω), and the shadow of bodies, and in art the figures in paintings, and other things of that kind. Likeness, but not of every kind, appears to be the cause of falsehood. For this reason everything that is free of some likeness of the true is not false. The predestinations of Gottschalk are proved to have no likeness to the true; therefore they are not false. But what they are I cannot discover: for they are nothing. But who can discover nothing? Therefore they are found to be fabulous, for indeed that is fabulous which is neither true nor like the true, like the flight of Daedalus, which did not and could not have come about.[18]

2. There is also the other argument which is described as from effects to cause, by which it is proved that two predestinations are not of God. Of this argument the most important proposition is: of all things that are mutually opposed the causes must necessarily be mutually opposed. Reason forbids that one and the same cause can produce different and mutually opposed effects. What is the opposite of being if not non-being? What the opposite of life if not to die? What of justice if not sin? What of happiness if not unhappiness? If therefore it is clear that all these are mutually opposed, it follows also that their causes are mutually op-

---

17. Cf. Augustine, *Soliloquia* II, *passim* for the rest of this passage (*Soliloquies* NPN 7; FC 5; CC 6).

18. *Ibid.* 11, 19–20, and cf. *Periphyseon* V, 36 (*PL* CXXII, 962B).

Reason Does Not Permit of Two Predestinations

posed. For they cannot derive either from one cause or two of the same kind. Therefore, as the heretic affirms, if there are two predestinations in God, of which one, as he says, not only effects but by its violence even enforces life, that is being, and then justice, followed by happiness; and the second which is in every respect the opposite of the aforementioned, for from a different source it not only effects but even enforces sin, which is non-being, and then the destruction of death, which necessarily is followed by unhappiness; those two are mutually opposed. But if the divine nature, the highest cause of all the things that are, although it is simple and one, is most soundly believed to be multiple, it follows that it must be believed not to allow any division within itself. It remains therefore that in God there are not two predestinations which would effect as well as enforce mutual opposition. This cannot be. How can one believe that there is within the nature of God a cause that compels something by necessity—God, who made all that he made by the goodness of his will and the will of his goodness, whose goodness is his will and whose will his goodness?

3. There is not, then, a predestination such as to compel by its inevitable necessity life, justice, happiness, nor such as to compel the opposites of the aforementioned good things, namely death, sin, unhappiness. This reasoning is arrived at by the argument of the *enthymeme*, which is always from the opposite.[19] Its proposition is like this: God cannot be both the highest essence and not be the cause of those things only that derive from him. But God is the highest essence. He is therefore the cause of those things only which derive from him. Sin, death, unhappiness are not[20] from God. Therefore God is not the cause of them. The same syllogism can be put this way: God cannot be both the cause of those things that are and the cause of those things that are nothing. But God is the cause of those things that are. Therefore he is not the cause of those things that are not. Sin and its effect, death, to which unhappiness is conjoined, are not. Of them, therefore, neither God nor his predestination, which is what he himself is, can be the cause.

4. But when, in your heresy, you had already begun to make faulty and ill-considered assertions and toiled insolently in your pride to defend

---

19. Cf. the commentary by Boethius (*PL* LXIV, 1142D–1143A) on Cicero's *Topica* 13, 55.
20. Cf. Augustine, *De moribus* . . . II, 2, 3. (*The Catholic and Manichaean Ways of Life* E 5; NPN 4; FC 56).

TREATISE ON DIVINE PREDESTINATION

two predestinations, you were shown to have scant authority and retreated from your first assault. And because you were overborne by the plainest truth you lay low, and in lying low you kept silence, and in silence you devised later schemes worse than the earlier. So the result is that in you is fulfilled the reproach of the wicked, as it is written: "And the last error shall be worse than the former."[21] For, just as it does not trouble you to deny that you proclaimed two predestinations, which, however, you are clearly proved by many people to have done, so you are not ashamed a second time to pronounce that it is one but double. You write in the ravings of your confessions, or rather of your perfidy, as if you wished to defend the source of your error, namely the opinion of Isidore:[22] There is a twin predestination, either of the elect to rest or of the condemned to death. This you explain as follows: He does not, indeed, say there are two, because there are not, but twin, that is divided in two. Can it be, you shameless man, that now that you are weak and enfeebled, abandoned by all the help of truth, you are reviving the war of words, trying to distance yourself stealthily from your first shamelessness, as if it should be more acceptable and less opposed to the truth to declare God's predestination twin, that is divided in two, rather than two? You strive to prove this twinning or division in two by the example of charity. So, you say, is predestination called twin,[23] namely divided in two, that is for the elect and the damned, whereas it is one, although it is double, just as charity or love is called twin, while being not at all two but one, although double, that is to say towards God and towards one's neighbour.

5. Oh how truly it has been said of you: From the locust shall come forth the wingless locust.[24] From your blasphemy against predestination has emerged your blasphemy against charity, so that the punishment for the former sin is the sin that follows. And so you seem to have the same faith in charity as you profess concerning predestination: for you maintain that each of them is double. You do concede, unless I am mistaken, if you are not out of your mind, that God is charity, as the passage of scripture asserts which says: God is charity.[25] You have not dared to deny that

---

21. Matt. 27.64.
22. Isidore, *Sententiae* II, 6, I (*PL* LXXXIII, 606A).
23. *gemina*.
24. *Bruc(h)us* is variously rendered in biblical translations as wingless or bald locust, or cankerworm. The reference here is enigmatic but suggests a deteriorating situation. Cf., *e.g.*, Joel 1.4; Ps. 104.34.
25. 1 John 4.8 and 16.

Reason Does Not Permit of Two Predestinations

predestination is God as you have openly professed in your confessions: for you wrote that his predestination was coeternal with God. And would that you consulted the Truth in the other things you have said about predestination, as you did on the question of its coeternity with God. Therefore there is agreement between us on charity and predestination, in that charity is God and predestination is God and one God, one divine essence, eternal and immutable. Accordingly if charity and predestination are predicated essentially of God, and no catholic doubts that essence is the highest unity and the true charity, so predestination is unity. If it is unique and immutable it must be devoid of number although from it are all numbers: if it should be devoid of mutability, it cannot be multiplied. The first multiple is double; therefore unity is not double, for it is the divine substance. There is no doubt that predestination is predicated essentially of God; but essence is unity; therefore predestination is unity. Unity is not double; therefore predestination is not double; and for that reason it is not twin either. How indeed should there be a twinship where there is no number or plurality? Divine unity is devoid of numeral plurality; therefore it is devoid of doubleness.

Of the same kind is reasoning about division in two. If predestination is most correctly predicated of the unity of the divine substance, and all true unity is free of parts, therefore predestination is not divided in two because it is not composed of parts. Indeed just as the divine nature is also not susceptible of *genera* and their forms, differences and numbers, although it is the cause of all of them, so also it is free of any composition of all the parts by which they are made up, although it is the author of the whole of each. With what impertinence, then, do you not hesitate to proclaim predestination, which is God, and charity to be divided in two, adding the explanation: that is double? Accordingly, just as none of the faithful dares to call God twin, or divided in two, or double, because it is impious, so also it is sacrilege to declare predestination and charity to be twin, or to double them or to divide them in two. For, whatever is believed of God must needs be believed also of his predestination and charity.

6. O eternal charity, how stricken with blindness are those who declare you to be double, and find that those who preach your word proclaim that you are twin, for they are unable to distinguish by intellectual insight the difference between you and your commandment. Your commandment, most powerful mistress, is said to be twinned because it is directed first towards you yourself, who are God, then towards our

neighbour since in him you also are loved. Indeed, nothing is loved in all respects, except love, which is you, single, undivided and immutable substance, and nothing loves completely except you, the indissoluble bond by which all things are held together.[26] Therefore you love; you are loved: and so your commandment is called twin, since partly you command that you be loved in yourself with no nature intervening, partly that you be loved in our neighbour with created nature interposed.[27] Is it on this account, then, o undivided unity, that we must believe you to be twin? Will our love be multiplied according to the number of things we love? Do we not love all things we love with the same love, while one and the same love is not evenly distributed among all—to some it is more adapted, to others less—yet it remains in itself without increase and without loss to its position. For we are not commanded to love God with one love and our neighbour with another, nor with one part of one to cleave to the creator, with the other to cleave to the creature, but with the whole of one and the same we must embrace both God and our neighbour. Therefore the precept of charity is twin, not charity itself, and in this way twin, because there is such a differentiation in the commandment that God should be loved on his own account but our neighbour not for himself on his own account but God's. Charity, then, loves God, that is itself, in all, and in it there is no twinship and for this reason no duplication

7. The argument of charity demonstrates, therefore, what we should accept concerning the twinship of predestination, which in the same way is in itself neither twin nor divided in two nor double, although there may appear some difference in its effects according to considerations of mercy and justice. For indeed, by one and the same predestination of his, a just and merciful God, powerful in all things, chose, out of the mass of human beings which was originally corrupted altogether, except for Christ, some to whom he had intended to give that which by their own agency they would not possess, that is his own gifts by which they would live. He abandoned some who by their own agency would contrive their own sins by which they would perish. To the former he gave the source of future happiness; to the latter he did not give, but permitted, the means by which in their unhappiness they would undergo punishment. For the

26. Cf. Augustine, *De trinitate* VIII, 8, 12.
27. Cf. *id.*, *De uera relig.* 55, 113; *De musica* VI, I, I (*On Music* FC 4); *De diuersis quaest. 83*, qu. 51, 2 and 4; *De Genesi ad litteram* 16, 60.

former it was not they, but he, who made preparation for life; for the latter it was not he, but they, who made preparation for death. For the former his merciful goodness was the cause of their supremacy; for the latter their own pride was the cause and effect of their torment.

Also the other incongruous examples that you accumulate to make predestination more complicated are indications more of your madness than of your error. Tell me, I pray you, by what reasoning did you take up the argument of dividing God's work in two to urge a double intertwining of predestination and charity?[28] While the work of God is numerous because it is created, yet just as predestination and charity are devoid of plurality, so are they also devoid of numerosity. Or, because the divine work, that is the universe of creatures, for example, is divided into two, as it were, principal species, namely spiritual and corporeal, are we for that reason obliged to duplicate predestination by which God arranged his future works? And if we are obliged, we shall necessarily be forced to believe in a quadruple also, since Augustine in his works says: "The divine work which created the world and governs it is distinguished by a quadriform system."[29] And the power common to all by which every thinking soul is formed will be quadrupled, since the condition of the soul expresses itself in four powers. As if from unity, although devoid of all species and parts, nevertheless every species and all parts should not originate! Or as if from the imprint of one signet-ring many marks could not be made on wax! What is it that you said about a fourfold world? O 'leaden dagger'![30] Or do you perhaps consider that predestination consists of two parts, in the manner in which the world is composed of four elements, although it is one? Likewise why are you raving about a twin tree? Or do you think that the simplicity of predestination is to be compared with the branches of trees? It seems to me that already you are wallowing and suffocating among those great vats[31] that you are ordering to be prepared for you. You deserve indeed to burn in oil and pitch, for you had no qualms about expounding false teachings on the light of love and the mystery of predestination.

---

28. Gottschalk (*Confessio prolixior*, ed. C. Lambot, Oeuvres p. 67, 15–17) had adduced *De ciuitate Dei* VIII, 6, where Augustine in turn has been reporting the opinion of Varro.

29. The quotation is from Bede, *De rerum natura* (PL 90, 187) and has not been found in Augustine.

30. Cicero, *De finibus* IV, 18, 48 and Augustine, *Soliloquia* II, 4, 5.

31. The metaphor comes from Gottschalk himself, *op. cit.* (ed. Lambot, p. 74, 28–33).

CHAPTER FOUR

The One, True and Only Predestination of God

1. It remains then to treat of the one, true and only immutable and eternal predestination of the divine all-powerful will which at no time and in no place is unfulfilled. But first something must be said about the particular character of that heresy which is slandering it. So then, this Gottschalkian heresy, if it can be called by such a name, takes a position midway between two other mutually opposed heresies, that is, between the one called Pelagian and the one which contradicts it; of these, one disparages the gift of divine grace, the other condemns freedom of choice. Indeed, the Pelagian sect sets such great value on the freedom of will of a rational nature that, without the gift of grace, it should adequately achieve the justice of man. But the opposing sect affirms the gift of freely given grace to such an extent that by its sole operation in man, every believer attains the pinnacle of justice, while any exertion of free choice is disparaged. Thus, as has been said, one despises the gift of grace, the other the gift of freedom of choice, both equal in their irreverence, but unlike in their doctrine. The one now in question, however, so placed midway between the two mentioned above, as if attached to the two mutually

opposed extremes, partly agrees with them, partly contradicts, and claims as peculiar to itself whatever it contends that they lack. For while it attempts to establish in the divine predestinations, as it would have it, the necessary and inevitable causes of all the virtues by which happiness is attained, and of the vices by which one is cast down into unhappiness, what does it seem to urge but the refutation of the gifts of God, that is, the free choice of the will and the help of grace, by both of which assuredly the completion of man's justice is both begun and achieved?

2. In short, this new sect agrees with the Pelagian in that it declares that a gift of freely given grace is of no advantage to man in the exercise of justice, but only the necessity of predestination is of advantage; it disagrees with it in that it has totally ruled out the power of free choice as having no force either for doing good or committing sin, shamelessly placing all these acts within the necessity of predestination. But, in that it strives to remove the desire for free choice, it appears to side with those opposed to the Pelagian, to which it again reverts when it agrees that gifts of divine grace are of no profit to man. And indeed they are not gifts if they are made not by will but by necessity, since it is well known to all, wise and foolish, that all gifts are both bestowed by the will of the giver and received by the will of the recipient. And this is a peculiarity of this heresy, which those between which it is placed midway are shown to lack. For the Pelagian considers that the power of free choice is sufficient without the assistance of divine grace, but its opponent considers that the gift of grace alone is sufficient to achieve justice without the exertion of free choice. But neither one of them has undertaken to say that the necessity of predestination turns men around either towards justly living a good life or impiously living a bad one. This delusive necessity of predestination remains, therefore, a peculiarity of this third heresy.

3. But all these poisonous darts of devilish irreverence are very easily repulsed by the secure defences of an impregnable faith. Accordingly let us employ that kind of reasoning which is called ΑΠΟΔΙΚΤΙΚΗ (apodeictic), first against those who either deny or doubt that grace is of God and has power to save the world. Not that our intention should be to disarm the Pelagians or those opposed to them on the other side but of equal wickedness—this has been adequately done by the holy fathers—but that the warding off of the heresy now in question may be a refutation of those two. For there is no doubt that from them it emanates. Those, therefore, who cannot envisage God's grace, let them envisage the salva-

tion of the world. For it is impossible that at the same time the salvation of the world exists and the grace of God does not exist. For if by the grace of God the world were not set free, how would its salvation follow? But the salvation of the world and the grace of God can both exist at the same time. Accordingly if the salvation of the world exists, necessarily grace will exist. But we hold most firmly that the salvation of the world has come. So let us hold most surely that the grace of God has shone forth. Let them hear the words of the apostle: "For the grace of God has shone forth."[32]

Next, a reply must be made in the same way to those who deny altogether the free choice of the human will or have some doubt about it. If you are unable to believe in free choice, you do not believe that there will be a judgment of the world. But if you cannot deny the judgment of the world, you are obliged to acknowledge free choice. For there is not both a judgment of the world in the future and no free choice now: these certainly cannot both coincide. For by what justice will there be judgment if there is not free choice? But one can state that at the same time there is both free choice and there will be judgment. If, therefore, there is judgment of the world in the future, there will necessarily be free choice of the will. But it is impious to deny that there will be a just judgment of the world. Therefore it is impious not to believe that free choice has been given to man by God. Accordingly the conclusion is that both the choice of man and the gift of grace are free, because it is conceded that the salvation of the world has come and there will be judgment. The king's highway must then be trodden with no turning aside to right or left,[33] which means that free choice must not be defended in such a way that good works are attributed to it without the grace of God; nor must grace be so defended that, as it were from the safety afforded by it, evil deeds may be habitually performed.

4. A response must, however, be made to this third heresy which the perverse thinking of Gottschalk has added on at the devil's inspiration. Indeed, there is no doubt that with diabolical subtlety it flows from the two forementioned heresies, although it may seem partly a denial of them, partly an admission. For one of those argues against free choice, the other against grace; but this man labours to dismantle at once both free choice

32. Titus 2.11.
33. Cf. Num. 20.17.

and the gift of grace. Therefore, in opposition to this we argue as follows. If someone cannot see, or rather is unwilling to acknowledge, that there is no inevitable or compulsive necessity within divine predestination forcing it, for instance, to act in some way on its creatures; and he cannot see that predestination is not itself a necessary cause which violently impels a rational being either to cleave to his God by holy living or wickedly to abandon his God, then that person should look at the free choice of the will and the gifts of grace. For there cannot at the same time exist free choice and the gift of grace side by side with the necessity of predestination. How indeed can there be in one both the necessary cause compelling and the voluntary cause effecting? For freedom, either of grace or of will, has no place where there is an unchangeable captivity of nature. But there are both possibilities that at the same time there exist free choice combined with the gift of grace, and there does not exist the necessity of predestination; for clearly freedom removes captivity. If, therefore, wherever there is freedom of choice with the gift of grace, there the necessity of predestination cannot be, it follows conversely that where there is the necessity of predestination, there neither free choice nor the gift of grace can be. But we very rightly believe and very clearly perceive that both free choice and the gift of grace can be in man. Let us therefore most faithfully understand that the necessity of predestination cannot be in man. For to every man freedom of his own will is universally given; yet not in every case, but only in those predestined, is it prepared, helped, secured, perfected and crowned by the gift of grace. But in none is it universally impelled or shackled by divine predestination, but is hindered by original and personal sin, through the secret yet just judgment of God.

5. To return, then, to true predestination: by its own guidance we most firmly believe and clearly see that it is single and solely substantial. For the true predestination of God which, before all the things were made which by it and through and in it were made, foresaw their making in measure and number and weight, and disposed that they would be made is truly God. For it is the willing cause and the causative will of all creatures, among which it created a rational creature to understand it, in order that it could enjoy its own highest good, that is, the contemplation of its creator. And it bestowed upon it its gift, namely that of free choice of its will, so that by using that gift well, that is by obeying dutifully and humbly the command of its creator, it would always justly and happily live. But if it used the same gift badly, that is, to abandon the highest

good, namely its creator, and to cling with perverse will to corruptible goods, unhappiness would duly follow as punishment. Most justly indeed does the impoverishment of the basest will pursue him who abandons the richest and most beauteous happiness. And so that very art[34] by which all things were made, that is, the highest and immutable wisdom of God, has by predestining so arranged the making of the rational creature as to impose upon it no necessity which would by an inevitable force compel it, although unwilling, to serve its God or to abandon him, though willing to cleave to him. For in the one case there would seem to be a captivity of created reason, in the other wickedness on the part of the creator. For in such a very just and most beneficent manner he had regard for the nature of the whole world, which he made to his own image and likeness, that it should serve him by will, not by necessity, indeed by the most just governance of divine wisdom. For rational life was bound not to have been made otherwise than voluntary, since by that will which is the cause of all things it was created in his own image and likeness. Otherwise how would the divine will, that is to say the highest reason of the universe, being unrestricted by any necessity as in the greatest freedom it possesses its own power, how could he make it to his own image and likeness if he did not create its substance a free rational will?

6. This is very clearly proved by the argument which is taken from the sin of the first man. For, although by sinning he cast away the life of happiness, he did not lose his substance which is to be, to will, to know.[35] For he is and he wills and he knows; he wills to be and to know; he knows that he is and that he wills. What, then, did the first man have before sinning that he lost after the sin? For up to then he did not have the life of happiness which was to have been bestowed on him if he kept the commandment. If we say it was free will he had, then he lost his nature. But if reason points out that no nature can perish, we are forbidden to say that he lost free will, which without doubt is a substance. For God did not create in man a captive will but a free one, and that freedom remained after the sin. For there is no sinful soul which does not desire happiness and does desire unhappiness. What more, then, did he have before the sin? For before he could commit sin, he had the wish to sin but did not wish to

---

34. Cf. Augustine, *De libero arbitrio* III, 15, 42 (*The Free Choice of the Will* ACW 22; CC 6; FC 59).
35. Id., *Confessiones* XIII, 11, 12 (*Confessions* numerous translations).

be made unhappy. But who dares to say that he did not wish to be made happy, since the desire for happiness still remains in the nature corrupted through him? Or perhaps by sinning he lost the strength of free will and the power by which on its own he could keep the commandment if he so wished? And in this way, the strength and the power of free choice was not in the first man by way of substance but by grace of the creator; he lost that great gift by wrongly exercising the free choice of the will. For he did not will to do what he was able to do, that is, to keep the commandment, which afterwards, being sinful, he is unable to do, even should he will it, without the help of grace.

7. Hence Augustine says in his book, *The Gift of Perseverance*:[36] "If, then, other proofs did not exist, the Lord's Prayer would alone suffice us in support of the grace which we are defending. For it leaves us nothing of which we can, as it were, in ourselves be boastful. Indeed it shows that our not departing from God must be the gift of God alone, since it shows that we must ask for it from God. For, whoever is not drawn into temptation does not depart from God. This is not at all within the power of free choice such as it now is. It had been so in man before the fall. Yet the great worth of this freedom of the will in the preeminence of that first creation was seen in those angels who, when the devil fell with his followers, remained steadfast in the truth and merited to attain to that perpetual state of assurance against falling in which we are now quite certain that they are. But after the fall of man, God willed that only by virtue of his grace should man come to him, and willed that only by virtue of his grace should man not depart from him. This grace he placed in him whose lot we have inherited, predestined according to the disposition of him who works out all things."[37] How then are we to understand Saint Augustine's words in the *Enchiridion* when he says: "By the misuse of free choice man lost both himself and it,"[38] unless perhaps we are to believe that he wished to point out by these words not that we should accept that the first Adam lost his substance, which he could not, but changed it to an inferior thing, which he could do? Certainly human nature was better at that time when it possessed the will and the ability, one by substance, the other by grace,

---

36. Id., *De dono perseverantiae* 7, 13-14 (*The Gift of Perseverance* E 15; CUA 91; NPN 5).
37. Eph. 1.11.
38. Augustine, *Enchiridion ad Laurentium* 9, 30 (*Faith, Hope and Charity* ACW 3; FC 4; CC 7; NPN 3).

than it is now when it has only the will without the ability, that is, nature bereft of the gift.

8. Hence the Lord in the gospel said to his disciples: "Without me you can do nothing";[39] he did not say: "you can will nothing"; and the apostle: "it is for me to will but not to accomplish."[40] Also as the same apostle says: "It is not a matter of willing or running but of God's mercy,"[41] which is understood in no other way but "although he is willing and running." For, by nature these two are implanted in man, since he wills and so he is willing, and seeks happiness and so he is running. Yet it is not the concern of a willing or running person to begin or perform or accomplish good works; for this is the gift of a merciful God. For, when a man is placed in very thick darkness, although he has the sense of sight he sees nothing, because he cannot see anything until light comes from outside; and when his eyes, hitherto closed but now opened, become aware of this, he catches sight of the light and in it all his surroundings. So the will of man, for as long as it is covered by the shadow of original sin and its characteristics, is hindered by its darkness. But when the light of divine mercy shines in, it dissipates not only the night of all sins and their guilt, but also by its healing it opens up the eye of a weak will, and, purifying it by good works, makes it fit to contemplate the light. But it is time to return to our subject.

---

39. John 15.5.
40. Rom. 7.18.
41. *Ibid.* 9.16.

CHAPTER FIVE

No One Is Compelled to Do Good or to Do Evil by the Foreknowledge and Predestination of God

1. And so in the present instance, since of all the evils of which God is not the originator the efficient cause is not necessarily predestination, as in my opinion is clearly proved also by the rules of reasoning, right order requires that we should take up our strongest arguments from the foreknowledge of God. By it we shall specifically show first how the foreknowledge of God does not compel to be committed the sins which it foresees, and so his predestination does not determine to be committed the sins which he never permitted. For if foreknowledge does not carry out all that it has foreseen, how can predestination accomplish all that it has not predestined? By his foreknowledge God foresees the future misdeeds of men; nevertheless, he is not the doer of them. We believe that he has not predestined the misdeeds of men by his predestination; how therefore can he be thought to be performing them? Why? Is one not mad to say that what God foreknows and does not do is done because of his predestination, seeing that he does not predestine it? If, then, God is both authoritatively believed and by reason seen to have known all sins in advance, but not to have committed them, nor to have predestined any of

them,—for how can there be one who commits sins while being also their destroyer and avenger?—is it not shameless folly, or rather villainy, to consider that by his predestination he enforces what he has not predestined, when by that same foreknowledge of his he does not enforce but permits?

2. Secondly, if authority is sought to demonstrate that God has foreknowledge of all evils though they are not from him, but yet that he is not their efficient cause, the words of the father Augustine alone suffice, from his third book of *On Free Choice:* "If I am not mistaken, you would not necessarily compel one to sin whom you knew would sin, nor would your foreknowledge itself compel him to sin, even if without doubt he was going to sin; for you would know that it would not be otherwise. Therefore, just as these two are not mutually opposed, your knowing by your foreknowledge what another by his own will is going to do, in the same way God, while compelling no one to commit sin, does nevertheless see in advance those who will sin of their own volition. Why, therefore, does his justice not punish what his foreknowledge has not enforced? Just as you by your recollection do not enforce what is past, so God by his foreknowledge does not compel to be done what is going to be done. And just as you remember certain things that you have done, and yet you yourself did not do all the things that you remember, so God has foreknowledge of all that he will do himself but is not himself the doer of all that he knows of in advance. But of those deeds of which he is not the evil doer, he is the just avenger. Hence you must now understand the justice by which God punishes sins, in that he does not perform those actions which he knows will take place. For if the reason he ought not penalise sinners is because he foresees that they will sin, he also should not reward the righteous because no less does he also foresee that they will act justly. Rather let us acknowledge that it is by virtue of his foreknowledge that nothing that is to be is hidden from him, and by virtue of his justice that sin, because it is voluntarily committed, does not go unpunished by his judgment, just as by his foreknowledge sin is not committed by compulsion."[42] "Such being the case it is very far from the truth that the sins of the creature are regarded as attributable to the creator—although necessarily that will take place which he has known in advance. So that when you said you cannot

---

42. *De libero arbitrio* III, 4, 10–11. The person addressed here is not Gottschalk but the interlocutor in Augustine's dialogue.

No One Is Compelled by Foreknowledge and Predestination

find a reason why whatever takes place in the creature should not necessarily be attributed to the creator, I, on the contrary do not find a means (and I affirm that none can be discovered, or exists at all), by which to attribute to him whatever has to take place in his creature, in such a way that it takes place by the will of sinners."[43] "Therefore I do not find, and I assert that there cannot be found, nor does there exist any way at all by which our sins may be attributed to God our creator, since I find him to be praiseworthy even in them, not only because he punishes them but also because they are committed precisely when his truth is abandoned."[44]

3. For this reason it must be declared very firmly that it is not possible at the same time that God's foreknowledge of the sins which he permits in his creature, by which he knows them in advance does not cause them, but his predestination which did not predestine them does cause them. But whatever is deduced concerning sin, whether general or specific, must also be regarded as true of its punishment. The punishment of sin is death. Therefore what is said of sin must be said of death. I do not speak of every death but only of that which follows sin. For we say that we die by sin, that is, for the offence of sin we die. Also we say that we die to sin[45] when, freed from sin, we live to justice. If, then, the cause of every sin is determined neither in God's foreknowledge nor in his predestination, it is very clear that the cause of every death that follows sin is not in God's foreknowledge, and it is equally certain that likewise the cause is not in his predestination. This is true even though spiritual writers, by a certain kind of misapplied terminology, are in the habit of speaking of persons predestined to death or destruction or punishment. Of this we shall speak later, as the Lord reveals.

4. Meanwhile we must consider if, just as God neither by foreknowledge nor predestination compels anyone to sin, similarly he compels no one to live righteously. In this matter it must be understood that there is no true freedom of any will if some cause has imposed compulsion. Therefore if some cause precedes a human will which by force compels it, though unwilling, towards good or evil thoughts or actions, it follows not only that it is not truly free but that it is not free at all. For wherever there is a compelling cause, there is not present a nature which

---

43. *Ibid.* III, 6, 18.
44. *Ibid.* III, 16, 46.
45. Cf. Rom. 6.2 and 10.

wills. But human nature is not only a will but also a free one, and its freedom is not false but true, although that freedom is so vitiated after sin that its punishment impedes it from either willing to live righteously, or should it so will, from so doing. From this unhappy state it is set free, as the apostle says,[46] by the grace of God through Jesus Christ, although its natural freedom still remains, which is recognised in the desire for happiness implanted in it by nature.

5. One must, then, in no way concede that any compelling cause either good or bad precedes the will of man or of any other rational nature, lest the reward of its freedom be taken from it, whether good, if one has lived well with the assistance of divine grace, or bad if one has lived badly in one's own irrational and perverse manner. Hence no cause constrains man to lead a good or a bad life. For God is neither the necessary cause of all good things as fire is of burning, sun of heating or lighting, nor the compelling cause, as inclination is of sleeping, thirst of drinking; but he is the voluntary cause in the same way as wisdom is the cause of the wise man, sight of the seeing man, reason of the reasoning man. But conversely, although the cause of all evils is the perverse emotion of a rational substance misusing the free choice of its will, it is nevertheless not the necessary cause, as sin is of death, death of unhappiness, nor the compelling cause, as suffering is of pain, pain of sorrow; but it is voluntary, as desire is of avarice, avarice of fraud.

6. Here we must answer those who, refusing if not contemptuous of the correcting of their faults, and critical of the workings of God, are in the habit of asking insolently:[47] "Why did God give man a free choice by which alone it is proved that he sins? Would it not have been better if he had made him in such a way that he could not sin?" This they also try to infer, by a quite false sophism,[48] from the following proposition: "If free choice is the gift of God, but every gift is good, no gift is harmful, therefore free choice is not harmful. But how should free choice not be harmful when by it we sin? Or how can the gift of God be seen as an occasion of sin? God, rather, ought not to have given any occasion of death. God indeed ought to have made man such that he would not sin, since he could

---

46. Rom. 7.25.
47. Cf. Augustine, *op. cit.*, III, 19, 53 and 6, 18; *De Genesi ad litteram* XI, 7, 9; *Contra aduersarium legis et prophetarum* I, 14, 18–20 (PL 42).
48. *Paralogismus*.

No One Is Compelled by Foreknowledge and Predestination

have done so. For it is better not to be than to be in a state of unhappiness." This perverse view is easily confuted by turning to reason. They must be asked: "But if you are not afraid to refer responsibility for all your sins to the creator, why are you afraid to sin? Is it because you do not want to die? Is God then unjust—perish the thought—when he punishes the sins for which he has given the opportunity? Free choice is not, then, the cause of sins, since it is the gift of God."

7. Then they should be asked: "Why are you afraid of dying? Is it because you want to live?" For the reason above all why death is to be feared is that it takes away the life either of the body or of the soul or of both. But if you want to live, say whether happily or unhappily. There is no one who wants an unhappy life. Nevertheless the happy life is nothing if it is attained by a will subject to compulsion, or it is possessed without freedom. Or, if God had not given free choice to man by which to desire happiness and purify himself by the good works through which it would deservedly be restored to him, how would God justly crown with the glory of happiness one who was unable to serve him of his own volition?

8. But you may ask: "Why did God, when he could have, not give man such a free choice that he would have no wish other than to live dutifully and justly, and could have no other wish, and indeed would have neither the wish nor the ability to live wickedly or unjustly?" I will answer you at once: "If God had created such a will in man, that it was not in every way self-moving either righteously or perversely, it would not be in every way free, but only partly free, partly unfree, free indeed to live justly but not free to live unjustly. If, therefore, there was some partial necessity, it would not be complete freedom. Or how of the same will could it be said simultaneously: 'it is free,' 'it is not free'? For these statements are contradictory because they cannot occur simultaneously. For if it is true to say that 'it is free,' it is false to say that 'it is not free'; but if it is true to say that 'it is not free,' it is false to say that 'it is free.' And for this reason free choice could by no means stand its ground if in any respect it was defective." You may ask: "what harm would come to man if his free choice was in part defective, that is to say he could not misuse it, and only to the extent that by using it well he would attain to eternal life? For it is better to live happily than to have full freedom of the will." Your blindness is to be marvelled at, and even more to be pitied. Is it possible that you do not know what justice is? Certainly you don't. For if you did know you would surely remain silent. Listen, then, to what justice is. It is de-

fined as follows: "Justice is to give every man his due." Therefore if no one can cast aside the justice of God, desist from ranting at it. How in fact does God, the just judge, give the crown of life to a man except to one dutifully serving him? But who serves God dutifully if not the man who keeps his commandments? And who keeps God's commandments if not he who shrinks from what he forbids him to do, and strives for what he commands, and hastens to do it by the help of his grace without which he can accomplish no good? But what does he forbid except sinning, or what does he command except not to sin? It would be superfluous, however, for man to be forbidden to commit sin if he did not possess the power freely to commit it. For what is impossible is not forbidden. Or on what account would he be commanded not to sin, if he was in no way able to sin? For God had to command what man was capable of doing. But in what way God wished to command what man could not do, I do not see. If, indeed, as you would have it, God were to have created free choice of such a kind in man that thereby he was only able not to sin but was not able thereby to sin, in what way then did he prohibit one course of action, that is to sin? For even if he had not made the prohibition, that would not be which in contravention of the law of nature could not be. But in what way did he command another course of action, that is not to sin, when indeed if it were not commanded to happen, it would necessarily have been so? For if man could not sin under the impulse of a natural force, by what means would he sin?

9. By this reasoning, therefore, it is shown both that God gave the first man such a will and that he created it in him free, to the extent that by means of it he was able to sin, just as he was able to die and was able not to die. Accordingly, the original command was fixed midway between sinning and not sinning. Indeed he forbade the one which was possible by the freedom of nature; the other he commanded, which he acknowledged to be possible by nature and grace, so that if he wished to obey it he would justly obtain happiness, but if on the other hand he disdained it, he would justly undergo the merited death and subsequent unhappiness. This being so, no christian person should doubt that God the creator of the universe has given man free choice, that is the option either of good or of evil, and that he could not fittingly have given it otherwise than totally free. Thus he would demonstrate what efficacy nature had in man without grace, what power grace had in nature, what the reward of justice, what of sin, what finally the gift of his ineffable generosity. Consequently, if anyone

No One Is Compelled by Foreknowledge and Predestination

were to disparage freedom of choice, either by belittling it or by totally sweeping it aside, or by blasphemy against it, both divine and human authority would prove him beyond doubt to be hostile to the whole of christian teaching.

Hence Augustine, in his treatise *On True Religion*:[49] "But if that defect," he says, "which is called sin, like a fever overtook one against his will, the punishment would rightly seem unjust which overtakes the sinner and is called damnation. But now to such an extent is sin a voluntary evil that by no means would sin exist if it were not voluntary, and this is indeed so obvious that none of the few who are learned, or the mass of the unlearned, would disagree on it. It must, therefore, either be denied that sin is committed, or acknowledged that it is voluntarily committed. No one can rightly say that a soul has not sinned who admits that it is corrected by repentance, and that pardon is given to the penitent, and that he who persists in his sins is condemned by the just law of God. Finally, if it is not by will that we do wrong, no one at all should be rebuked or warned; without these strictures the christian law and all the system of religion is of necessity swept aside. Therefore, it is by will that sin is committed; and since there is no doubt that sin is committed, I do not see that it can be doubted that souls also possess free choice of the will; for God judged that such servants of his would be better if they served him freely, which would be quite impossible if they served him not by free will but by necessity."

---

49. Augustine, *De uera relig.* 14, 27.

CHAPTER SIX

Every Sin Has No Other Source Than the Free Choice of the Individual Will

1. It is very firmly to be maintained, then, that no sin, that is, no evil deed, and no punishment for it, has its origin elsewhere than in the individual will of man who misuses the freedom of choice. And true reason does not find it to be otherwise. In order to demonstrate this, use must be made of the argument by comparison. If the will is according to nature human, from this it is very foolish to doubt, and no one does doubt, that it is not the highest will of all, this principally from the evidence that it is changeable. For if it were the highest of all, how could it be changeable? It is not, then, the highest. But since we see that it shares in the highest reason, we cannot doubt that it is a rational substance. Secondly, if rational nature deservedly takes precedence over irrational, it follows that a changeable rational nature is inferior to an immutable rational one, but greater than an irrational and changeable one. We must, then, believe that the divine will, the highest of all, in no way has either urged the rational will, which it created, to sin, or compelled it to sin. But how could an irrational will, like that of the animals, overcome a will better than itself, especially as it cannot sin itself, being devoid of reason? How could it

have either urged or compelled to sin a will stronger than itself, one indeed making use of reason?[50] There remains on a par with it a will, if such exists, which is either free from vice or is vitiated. But if it were to be free from vice, by what means can it either urge or enforce vicious actions in a will equal to itself? For no will that is free from vice effects vice in another will. But if it is vitiated it is not on a par with the human will before sin. For every will free of corruption is better than one not free of it. The conclusion is that every opportunity for evil doing and all punishment for it is in man's own will.

2. Hence Augustine, in the first book of *On Free Choice*:[51] "It remains, therefore, that for the mind that is in control and in possession of virtue whatever is equal to or more highly esteemed than itself cannot make it the servant of lust, because of its justice; but whatever is inferior cannot do so through weakness, as is indicated by the points we have settled between us: hence nothing else makes the mind a companion to cupidity except its own will and free choice, and justly it pays the penalties for such great sin. What then? Is it to be considered a slight penalty that lust holds sway over it, and drags it, despoiled of its wealth of virtue, poor and needy in different directions? At one moment it approves the false as if it were true. At another it is on the defensive. Now it rejects what it had previously approved and yet seizes upon other falsehoods. Now it suspends its own assent, and often fearful of the clearest reasonings, despairs altogether of finding the truth, being deeply attached to the darkness of folly. Now it strives for the light of understanding, and again for weariness falls back. Meanwhile that dominion of the passions tyrannically rages and by changing and conflicting storms disturbs man's whole mind and life; from one side by fear, from the other by longing; from this side by anxiety, from that side by an empty and false joy; from one side by the torment of some beloved object lost, from the other side by eagerness to acquire things not possessed; from this side by the pain of injustice suffered, from that by the stimulus of revenge. Whatever way it turns, avarice can constrain it, extravagance waste it, ambition fasten on to it, pride inflate it, envy torture it, sloth overwhelm it, inflexibility provoke it, subjugation shatter it, and all the other countless things which crowd into and disturb

---

50. Cf. Augustine, *De libero arbitrio* I, 10, 20.
51. *Ibid.* I, 11, 21–22; I, 16, 34–35: in this instance Eriugena has adapted the text to exclude the interlocutor (see n. 42 above).

that realm of lust. Can we, finally, regard as no punishment that which, as you see, all who do not cleave to wisdom will have to undergo? But it is certain that what each one chooses to pursue and to embrace is settled within the will, and that by nothing except the will is the mind deposed from its citadel of rule and from its proper course, and it is manifest that, when someone misuses it, it is not a thing but the person who uses it badly that is to be blamed."

3. "On that account our attention may now be turned to consider if evildoing is anything else than neglecting eternal things, which the mind of itself enjoys and of itself perceives and which loving it cannot lose, to pursue, as though they were great and marvellous, things that are temporal and perceptible through the body, the lowest part of man, and which can never have an assured existence. For it seems to me that all evil deeds, that is sins, are contained within this one class, when anyone turns away from divine things and what is truly abiding, and turns towards the changeable and uncertain. Although those things are properly placed within their own order and achieve some beauty of their own, yet it is characteristic of a perverse and disordered mind to be overwhelmed by pursuit of them, when by the law of God and by right it is set above them for them to do its bidding."

CHAPTER SEVEN

Free Choice of the Will Should Be Reckoned among the Good Things That God Bestows on Man, although He May Misuse It. What Is It That Causes Sin and Is Sin?

1. Free choice, therefore, is not an evil, although each man may use it badly, but it is to be counted among the benefits which are conferred on man by divine bounty, especially as it was given rather to be used well. It is in this respect that human will is most seriously to be censured, in that it preferred to use wrongly the gift which was given to it to use rightly. But the question deserves to be asked: why was it able to use it badly? The reply is: because it is not a great good which nobody can use badly. For there are great goods which are bestowed by God on man; there are moderately great ones; there are ones of very little value. And in fact no one misuses the great ones. For who can misuse prudence, temperance, fortitude, justice? But by means of the moderately great good things and the least ones, both good and bad lives are led, according to the choice of the user. Someone skilled, for example, in the art of disputation that is called dialectic, which as no one doubts was bestowed by God on man, can if he

wishes make good use of it, since for that purpose it most certainly was given. While by it he instructs those who have no understanding of it, he distinguishes truth from falsehood, separates what is mixed up, brings together what is split apart, and in all things searches out the truth. On the other hand he can behave destructively, which was not the purpose of the gift, while in confirming false as true he directs others into error, and confuses the perception of the simple by false reasonings, and in confusing them darkens their understanding, preventing their inner eye, which is the mind, from attaining to the knowledge of the pure truth itself. Therefore, just as by that art, if it were counted among the great goods, no one would deceive or no one be deceived; similarly if free choice were placed among the number of the great goods, firstly no one misusing it would begin to fall, and none in consequence would be punished for misusing it. But who is there who cannot see men in great numbers misusing good things which, though of the smallest degree, yet were entrusted to them by God, such as bodily forms and their beauties which the majority of men use in a deadly way to satisfy their various passions, when they might use those same gifts dutifully, justly and rightly, to earn their own happiness, if they referred them back to the praise of the creator?

2. But to establish these matters more clearly the sweet-toned words of the holy father Augustine must be set forth. For he says in the second book of *On Free Choice:* "It is agreed between us that the nature of the body is of an inferior rank to the nature of the mind, and on that account mind is a greater good than body. If then in the good things of the body we find some such that man can improperly use them, and yet we do not say that for that reason they should not have been given to him, since we acknowledge that they are good, why wonder if in the mind too there are certain good things which we could also use improperly? But things which are good could not have been given except by him from whom all good things derive. For you see how much good is wanting in a body from which the hands are missing, and yet the hands are misused by any man who by means of them performs cruel or shameful acts. If you looked at someone with no feet you would admit that a very great good is missing from the wholeness of the body, and yet you will not deny that a man misuses his feet who uses his feet to injure anybody or to bring dishonour on himself. With the eyes we see this light of day and distinguish between forms of bodies, and that is the most beautiful thing there is in our body; and hence these members of the body are set as it were at the pinnacle of

Free Choice among the Good Things although Man May Misuse It

dignity, and use of the eyes is important for attending to our safety and for the many other advantages of life. Yet with the eyes many people perform many shameful acts and force them into the service of lust. And you see how much good is missing in a face if the eyes are missing. But when they are there, who has given them if not God, the bestower of all good things? Therefore, just as you approve those things in a body and, disregarding those who misuse them, you praise him who gave these good things, so you may admit that the free will without which no one can live rightly must be good and divinely given, and that they are to be condemned who misuse this good rather than that he who gave it ought not to have done so."[52]

3. "The virtues, then, by which life is rightly lived, are great goods; but the forms of any bodies, without which life can be rightly lived, are the least of goods; but the powers of the mind without which life cannot be rightly lived are intermediate goods. No one misuses the virtues, but the other goods, that is the intermediate and the least, each man can use not only well but also badly. And thus no one uses the virtues badly, because the work of virtue is the good use of those things which we could also not use well. But no one makes use of something badly by using it well. Therefore the richness and vastness of God's goodness guarantees not only the great goods but also the intermediate and the smallest. His goodness is to be praised more in the great than in the intermediate, and more in the intermediate than in the smallest goods; but more in them all than if he had not given all."[53]

4. "The will, therefore, cleaving to the universal and unchangeable good, obtains man's first and great goods, although it is itself a sort of intermediate good; but a will sins that is turned away from the unchangeable and universal good and is turned towards the individual good or to something external or to something inferior. It turns towards its private good when it wants to have control of itself; to something external when it is eager to know what is particular to others or whatever does not pertain to itself; to something inferior when it loves the pleasure of the body. And so man, having become proud and inquisitive and licentious, is captivated by another kind of life which, compared with the higher life, is death. Yet it is governed by the direction of divine providence which

---

52. Augustine, *De libero arbitrio* II, 18, 48.
53. *Ibid.* II, 19, 50.

appoints all things to their suitable places and apportions to each man his due according to his deserts. And so it happens that those good things that are sought after by sinners are in no way bad, nor is free will itself, which we have found was to be counted among certain intermediate goods, but what is bad is its turning away from the unchangeable good and turning towards changeable goods; yet since this turning-away and turning-towards is not forced but voluntary, the deserved and just punishment of unhappiness follows after it."[54]

5. "But since the will moves when it turns away from the unchangeable good to the changeable good, you are perhaps going to ask where the movement originates from, as it is certainly evil, even if free will, without which it is impossible for life to be rightly lived, is to be numbered among the good things? For if that movement, that is the turning away of the will from the lord God, is without doubt sin, surely we cannot say that God is the author of sin? That movement therefore will not be from God. From where then will it be? If you should ask such a question and I were to answer that I do not know, perhaps you will be somewhat downcast; but nonetheless my answer would be the truth. That which is nothing cannot be known. Only hold fast to your unshaken piety so that no good thing may in any way present itself to your feelings or your understanding or your thought that does not come from God. For thus no nature presents itself which is not from God; do not hesitate to attribute to God the creative artist everything in fact in which you see measurement and number and order. Hence if you totally withdraw those, nothing at all will remain. For even if some rudimentary kind of form did remain where you find neither measurement, nor number, nor order—for wherever those are there is perfect form—one must also remove that rudimentary form which appears as a kind of raw material awaiting the finishing touch of the creative artist. For if the perfection of form is a good, already the rudimentary form is something good also. Thus if every good is totally withdrawn, absolutely nothing will remain. But every good thing is from God; therefore there is no nature that is not from God. Take note, then, of that movement of turning away which we acknowledge to be sin because it is a defective movement, and every defect comes out of nothingness. Take note of where it belongs and have no doubt that it does not belong to God. Yet

---

54. *Ibid.* II, 19, 53.

Free Choice among the Good Things although Man May Misuse It

that defect, because it is voluntary, is placed within our power. For if you fear it, your duty is not to will it; but if you do not will it, it will not be. What then is more secure than to be in that life where nothing can happen to you that you do not will? But since man, though he fell by his own will, cannot in the same way rise, let us with a firm faith grasp the right hand of God stretched out to us from above, that is our lord Jesus Christ, and with sure hope await him and with burning charity long for him."[55]

---

55. Augustine, *De libero arbitrio* II, 20, 54.

CHAPTER EIGHT

The Difference between Man's Nature and His Free Choice

1. Now is the time to knock on the door of God's mercy that he may deign to unlock for us the difficulty of a pressing question. Far removed indeed and stored away in the secret recesses of deep intelligence is the question of the difference between man's free will, which comes from nature, and his free choice which, without doubt, is manifestly a gift of the creator. As indeed Saint Augustine many times very clearly impresses upon us, it is our belief that the substantial trinity of the interior man is composed of these three, namely being, will and knowledge.[56] For if the highest wisdom which wished to create human nature like itself is in itself one and three, it duly made man in that way, that is being, will and knowledge, for those three are one. Indeed, for the rational life being is not other than willing, nor willing other than knowing, but its being is a knowing will and its will a knowing essence and its knowledge a willing essence.

2. These three, therefore, are one and one nature. The whole nature of the soul, then, is will. But one must consider whether that will just as it naturally exists, similarly is naturally free, or only has its existence as

---

56. Cf. Madec edition p. 48: this particular triad is not to be found among numerous triads adduced by Augustine in his writings.

will from nature but is free by gift of the creator. In fact while every good thing either is God himself or is something from him,[57] nonetheless we do not say that all good things that are from him are made by him in the same way. In fact, of all the good things which God created some are out of his goodness, but some out of his generosity. But those that are made by his goodness are made substantially with all the accidents which naturally adhere to them, which are qualities, quantities, relations, situations, conditions, places, times, action and passion; within that ten in number all created substance as well as all accidentals to it can be included. Let us not be disturbed if those things are called accidents which are not from nature: for they are not truly accidents, but either the absence or the deficiency of natural accidents, that is corruptions. But those things which come through the generosity of the creator are truly called his gifts and should not be believed to be otherwise, because some three components are necessarily to be understood in every act of giving—the giver, the gift and the receiver.

3. Accordingly God, who fashioned all things, first in his goodness created the substances of the universe he was to create, and then in his generosity arranged to bestow gifts on each according to its rank. Manifestly, among those substances, he brought into being[58] the nature of man under the control of a rational will. For man is not a will for the reason that he is will, but because he is a rational will. Indeed, take away the will and there will not be a man. Yet the converse does not hold that if you were to take away the man there would not be a rational will, for this is recognised not in man only but also in an angel and in God himself. Hence the necessity to consider what that human will possesses by nature, what by virtue of the gift. But if it is clearer than daylight that it owes to nature the fact that it is a substantial will, it remains to be asked whence comes its freedom. For it is not absolutely called will but free will. If, then, from its creation it were to have its existence only as a will, but not a free one, it remains, if it is free—and to deny this would be absurd—that the freedom was bestowed on it as the gift of its creator. And the difference between nature and free choice will be such, as if the human will in its creation received not only its existence but also its freedom.

---

57. Cf. Augustine, *De libero arbitrio* III, 13, 36; *De uera relig.* 18, 35.
58. *Substituit:* in this same passage Eriugena twice uses the word *substitutio* to indicate God's act of creation.

Difference between Man's Nature and Free Choice

4. So far the question proposed has not been elucidated. In fact from the above-mentioned arguments it is inferred that the all powerful divine will, which is not restricted or obstructed by any law, was bound to create a will like its own, which would govern by the eternal laws of that creative will and should by no force be limited in acting as it wished, or compelled to act as it did not wish. Indeed whatever it would have preferred to do, either good or bad, should not exceed the wise discipline of its own creative power which would lend an ear to all the movements of the free will, whether right or wrong, in harmonious succession. For it is not to be believed that the creator of the universe made the rational will servile. Or does man perhaps not possess reason substantially? Who would dare to say so, since the true definition of man is: "Man is a rational substance receptive of wisdom"! Why wonder, then, that the human will of its nature possesses freedom, since it is not a wonder that it possesses reason? Or how could the will, to which that future freedom is deservedly promised for its obedience, have been made servile by nature because there will be no will to sin? For in no way, indeed, did God destroy that which in nature he created, but certain natural good things that he created he turned to further advantage, not so as to root out from them what he had made, but to add on to them what he wished to add over and above.

5. Take, for example, the human body before sin which was first animal, later to be spiritual[59] by virtue of obedience, without death intervening. Why first animal? Was it because up to this point there was missing that which was to be added on for keeping the commandment, that is to say the spiritual? And in this way, it was animal due to the fact that it fell somewhat short of the perfection of nature; it would be spiritual due to the fact that it had no shortcomings. From this, one is given to understand that the first will of man was created naturally free so that something nevertheless should be added to it if it wished to keep God's commandment. And just as the animal body was capable of dying because it was not yet perfect, so the free will, hitherto rightly animal because mortal, could sin since it was not yet perfect. Which perfection of freedom would assuredly be fulfilled after the keeping of the commandment, when that will to sin would be totally taken away, forming a will like that

---

59. Cf. Augustine, *De Genesi ad litteram* VI, 19, 30–28, 39; *De bono coniugali* 2, 2 (*The Good of Marriage* FC 27; NPN 3). Augustine contrasts the term 'spiritual' (*spiritale*) with the animal. The Madec and Floss (*PL* CXXII) texts retain *spirituale*.

future will which our lord Jesus Christ will give to those who love him. But, to strengthen this argument, let us use that method of reasoning which is taken from the lesser to the greater. If by nature we have a sense in our bodily eyes so that we are free to use their light to look at either honourable things or shameful, why wonder if God had created a will in man that would use its natural freedom honourably if he did not sin, or shamefully if he did sin? Therefore, why would not that which naturally applies to our body also apply to our soul, especially as where there is rationality, there necessarily will be freedom? But the human will is substantially rational. It is, therefore, substantially free.

6. This being so, more diligent consideration must be given to the question of what free choice is. This, without doubt, was bestowed by God on human nature. We are accustomed in the same words to describe both the substance of man and the gift, in such a way that there is some doubt as to what the words convey about the nature and what about the gift. What else do we understand when we hear of the free choice of the will except the impulse of the will, all of which express the nature of the human will. For the will is free, rational, subject to change. Or perhaps if it is changeable—which must by all means be admitted, if God alone is most correctly believed to be immutable—it may be asked whence it is changeable. To which the true answer is: whence free, thence changeable. But it is from nature that it is free. Therefore it is from nature changeable.

7. The next question asked is: whence is its movement? To which the answer is: from itself because it is free. Can it be from elsewhere? It can, because that will by which it is moved is greater and better than it. Which will is that? No other than the highest and divine one which created it and moves it. Can it be moved by an equal or lesser? It cannot. For if everything which causes movement is greater than the thing that is moved, of necessity greater things may not be moved by lesser. For similar reasons equal things cannot move their equals; for otherwise those moved would not be equal to those moving them; and for this reason equal things are moved by a cause stronger than themselves. It clearly remains that the human will is moved either by itself or by the will that created it. Well, since it is self-moving, can it be moved both rightly and wrongly? It is capable of both as it may wish, because it has free movement. What if it were to be moved by the one that created it, who would dare to doubt that it was being rightly moved? Accordingly, because the enquiry is con-

cerned with man's will before the sin, it must be conceded that it was capable of its own motion both of wishing to turn towards God so as not to sin and to turn away from him in order to sin, but to be moved by the higher cause only so as not to sin.

If then, as the above examination by reason indicates, the natural motion of the human substance, by which clearly it first turned towards the knowledge and love of its God and then towards itself, is accepted as coming about from two causes, one superior, which is the common possession of all natures, but the other inferior, which is established in the human substance itself, what prevents us from referring all right motions of our mind to our creator who, although he moves himself without time or place, moves our created spirit through time without place, and moves our bodies through time and place?[60] Into our nature too he introduced a cause by which we could ourselves move freely, reasonably, voluntarily, towards the pursuit of those ends to which it had been intended that we should attain. That motion is rightly called the free choice of our will because it is subject to our control. For we would be able, according to our judgment, to direct it on the right course; we would also be able to restrain it. From whence, then, would we have such a motion and such ability if not from God who bestowed on us this property to be not the lowest good of our nature as well as a praiseworthy gift of the creator? To him we owe it to return inexpressible thanks not only for creating, by the abundance of his goodness, the nature of our mind as rational, free, voluntary and mobile, but also because by the favour of his bounty he arranged that we could move at our own pleasure rationally, freely and voluntarily. This movement is granted to no living thing apart from man. For if we are instructed to praise that nature from among the beauty of the natures which he created without rational freedom of the will,[61] how much more should we praise him for our own substance which he so endowed that it should of its own motion cleave to its creator, and, if it wished, could restrain that same motion, so as not to depart from him! Indeed if that motion did not occur within the particular control of the human will, who could live rightly, who finally would commit sin, since it was given that by means of it one might live well, and in no way for the purpose of living evilly?

60. Cf. Augustine, *De Genesi ad litteram* VIII, 20, 39.
61. Cf. Augustine, *De libero arbitrio* III, 5, 12–16, 46.

8. Here let us listen to Saint Augustine: "If man were some good thing and could not do right except when he willed it, he had to possess free will without which he would be unable to do right. For not because also sin is committed by means of it is it to be believed that God gave it for that purpose. The sufficient reason, then, why it had to be given is that without it man could not live rightly. But here it may be understood that it was given for the following reason, namely that if anyone used it to sin he would be punished by God, which would not be just if free will had been given not only to live rightly but also to sin. For how would he justly be punished who had used the will for that purpose for which it was given? But now when God punishes a sinner, what else does he seem to you to be saying except: 'Why did you not use free will for the purpose for which I gave it to you, that is to do right?' Furthermore, as to that good by which justice itself is valued for condemning sins and honouring righteous actions: how could it be so if man were lacking in the free choice of the will? There would be neither sin nor right action if it were not carried out by the will; and for that reason both punishment and reward would be unjust if man did not have free will. There had to be justice in both punishment and reward because this is one of the good things which are from God. Therefore God must have given man free will."[62]

In relation to those words we must see to it that no one confuses substance and motion when they hear the words free will, which is undoubtedly substantial. Our holy father Augustine, then, did use such a mode of expression in saying free will for that which is the movement or choice of the free will, and we are in the habit of using it when by means of substantial causes we express their effects. Hence there is a circumlocution of true reason for a circumlocution of true reasoning—for true reason is substantially in man, and its movement is reasoning—the hand for the work, the foot for walking, the tongue for words, and other examples of that kind.

9. Therefore, if I am not mistaken, by this round-about manner of drawn-out reasoning it is deduced that the causes of all right deeds, by which one attains the crown of just happiness, are placed within the free choice of man's will by means of the gratuitous and manifold gift of divine grace which prepares it and cooperates with it; but that the principal root of evil deeds, by which there is a headlong fall into the contumely of just

---

62. Cf. Augustine, *De libero arbitrio* II, 1, 3.

unhappiness, is fixed within the perverse movement of free choice at the devil's urging. How great, then, is the folly of those who most falsely represent the inevitable causes of such things and their compulsive necessities as being in divine predestinations, and most shamelessly assert this, and finally—which is greatly to be deplored—as a result of their error thrust themselves and those who agree with them downwards to destruction in perpetual death!

Therefore, whether such a difference be found between the free choice of man and his substance, so that by nature a truly free choice in the rational will is constituted in its freedom; or in the movement of the naturally free will; or in the gift of intelligence which is bestowed on all in common; or, as is thought more probable, all three combined—that is the free movement of the intelligence—are the mutual components of free choice, the reason for this is that, as the substance itself in which it is is threefold—for it exists and wills and knows—so it also is made threefold, free, moved, intelligent. Yet it is evident that every sin and the punishments for sin have drawn their origin from its perverse use, and that it thrives in every sinner, leading to an evil way of life.

CHAPTER NINE

Foreknowledge and Predestination Are Predicated of God, Not Properly but by a Similitude of Temporal Things

1. Already at this point a structured treatment of the main question requires us to consider whether, in the sacred writing both of holy scripture and the holy fathers, it is literally or in a transferred sense that God is said to have foreknown or to have predestined either the whole universe, which he himself created substantially, or whatever aspect of the divine administration is temporally to be seen in it, that is to say, in those things which he himself does, not in those he allows to happen. In the first place it is to be noted—since no expression is adequate to God[63]—that almost no speech-signs, whether nouns or verbs or other parts of speech, can be properly affirmed of God. How could sensory signs, that is signs connected with bodies, signify with clarity that nature which is far removed from all corporeal sense and scarcely attainable to even the purest mind since it transcends all understanding? Yet toilsome human reasoning,

---

63. Cf. Augustine, *De diuersis quaestionibus ad Simplicianum* II, qu. 2, I (CC 6).

rendered indigent after the sin of man, does make use of them, so that somehow the abounding sublimity of the creator may be believed and intimated. Besides, if all verbal signs are not according to nature but contrived by human convention, why wonder if they are not adequate to describe that nature which alone is truly said to be?

2. Hence, of the verbal signs which divine and human diligence uses in customary human speech to signify God himself or his administration in the created world, some are quasi-proper. There are examples of these, for instance, among the verbs: I am, he is, he was, to be; and among the nouns: essence, truth, virtue, wisdom, knowledge, design, and others of this kind. Since in our nature these signify what may be first and best, that is, substance itself and the best parts of it without which it cannot be immortal, i.e., the accidents, they are not incongruously referred to the one and best beginning of all good things, which is God. There are, however, other images not proper, that is metaphorical,[64] images which tend to come from three bases, namely likeness, contrariety, difference. Of the first basis examples are: 'To whom is the arm of the lord revealed':[65] and: 'Your hands have made me':[66] likewise: 'The eyes of the lord are over the just and his ears are directed to their prayers.'[67] Those are rightly called improper, since the divine substance is in every way devoid of such lineaments of bodily members. But certain things are not inappropriately predicated of it by similitude. For nature has located, as if in their proper place, the physical strength of the body in the arms, in the hands executive power, in the eyes sight, hearing in the ears. Divine power, then, and God's work, his vision also and generosity, are most fittingly called by the names of those locations. By way of example of the third basis, to signify immutable substance, there are those conditions taken from the disturbances of our minds, such as anger, rage, indignation, fear, sadness, and other conditions drawn from the basis of difference, of which no likeness to the divine nature is found, but for the sole necessity of expressing a meaning, they are used in an extremely remote transferred sense.

3. There remain those which are taken from the basis of contrariety. So great is their power to express meaning that by a sort of privilege of

---

64. *Aliena; translata.*
65. Isa. 53.1.
66. Job 10.8; Ps. 118.73.
67. Ps. 30.16.

their excellence they are rightly called by the Greeks *entimemata*, that is, concepts of the mind. For although everything that is produced by the voice is first conceived by the mind, nevertheless not everything that is conceived by the mind is seen to have the same power of signifying when it is infused into the ferment of the senses. Therefore, just as the strongest of all the arguments is that which is taken from the contrary, so of all the vocal signs the clearest is that drawn from that same basis of contrariety. Of those, some are stated as absolute, some as in relation. The form of the absolute one is: "I shall destroy the wisdom of the wise and shall reject the prudence of the prudent."[68] Which is correctly understood from its contrary, as if he said openly: "I shall destroy the folly of the foolish, I shall reject the imprudence of the imprudent." That is clearly understood from the words of the apostle when he says: "The wisdom of this world is folly before God."[69] Indeed, if all wisdom is from the lord God, for what reason shall God be understood to destroy what comes from him? But what is believed about wisdom is similarly to be believed about prudence. For God does not destroy any power in man; an example of this 'absolute' form cannot easily be found referring to God.

4. And this is not surprising since nothing is contrary to God except non-being,[70] because he alone it is who said: "I am who am";[71] but other things also that are said to exist do not entirely exist, because they are not what he is, and they do not entirely not exist, because they are from him who alone is being. Unless perhaps we were to say that those things which are said concerning our lord Jesus Christ according to the particularity of his humanity can likewise be said of his divinity, because of the inseparable unity of one person in two substances. But if that is not irrationally believed to be the case, let us see what is written in the law: "Cursed is every man who has hung on a tree."[72] This is without doubt said of Christ, who is above all things blessed forever.[73] For we who have merited the curse of death and slavery in the sin of the first man, have received in the justice of the second man the blessing of life and freedom. For, the curse that the Jews uttered against Christ hanging on the cross implies more of

---

68. 1 Cor. 1.19.
69. *Ibid.* 3.19.
70. Cf. Augustine, *De ciuitate Dei* XII, 2.
71. Exod. 3.14; cf. Augustine, *Confessiones* VII, 10, 16–11, 17.
72. Deut. 21.23; Gal. 3.13.
73. Cf. Rom. 9.5.

a blessing than a curse. This form of expression is drawn, then, from the basis of absolute contrariety, which the apostle also adopted when he said: "He who knew not sin committed sin on our behalf."[74] Who indeed doubts that sacrifice and sin are mutually opposed, since sacrifice is performed for no other reason than the abolition of sin? Christ is the universal victim for the sin of the whole world. Rightly, then, is he signified from the contrary by sin.

5. Next let us consider examples of the contrary by relation. Those are, indeed, said to be in relation because they come together in two bases, that is, likeness and contrariety. For, the same nouns or verbs are used partly by likeness, partly by contrariety, of which paradigms are foreknowledge and predestination when predicated of God. And first, then, we must observe that these and such like terms, whether nouns or verbs, cannot be properly predicated of God. For in that regard it might be said that God has foreknowledge of something by foreknowledge, or foreordains by predestination, when to him nothing is in the future, because he awaits nothing, nothing is past because for him nothing passes. In him, just as there are not distances of places, so there are no intervals of times. And because of this no right reasoning permits such terms to be understood of God with the claim to be literal. For, how can foreknowledge be said to be his for whom there are no future happenings? Just as no memory of his can properly be spoken of, since for him there is no past; in the same way no foreknowledge since there is no future. And yet it is said: "The just shall be in eternal memory."[75] But God has seen, has foreseen, has known, has foreknown all things that are to be done before they are done, in the same way that he sees and knows those same things after they are done because, just as he himself is always eternal, so the universe that he made is always eternal in him.

6. Concerning his predestination also the same ideas must be held, especially as all predestination is foreknowledge. By what right can it be called *pre*destination, that is *pre*paration, in him who had no interval of time beforehand in which to arrange what he would do, whose preparation did not come before the operation? Indeed for him there is no difference between preparing and doing, and as it is proper to man to prepare what he is going to do, so it is not proper of God to predestine what he will never do. But how would he be going to make anything, who made all

74. 2 Cor. 5.21.
75. Ps. 111.7.

things once and together? Or how did he not make all things who always possessed all things,⁷⁶ whom we believe always to have possessed his own Word, through whom all things were made and in whom all things unchangeably live, not only the things that have been but those that will be? And yet they *were* not in him, nor *will* they be, but only *are*, and they are all one. Accordingly, since it is in one mode that those things which were made by him are under him, and it is in another mode that those things are in him which he himself is, in regard to those things which are under him because they are created and disposed in their places and times, the terms of times and places become literally significant, but in regard to the things that eternally are in him they can be used metaphorically. And for this reason, just as it is improperly said of God that he has made or will make, so it is improperly said of God that he has foreknown, is foreknowing and will foreknow, and likewise that he has predestined, is predestining and will predestine.

7. The conclusion is, then, that foreknowledge and predestination are metaphorically applied to God on the basis of a similitude to temporal things. This basis would be understood from the contrary if temporal things were in the mode of contradiction set over against eternity. Now since some likeness of eternity is implanted in temporal things—not only because from it they were made but also because that part of the temporal from which these names are taken, that is, the human, will be transformed into some likeness of the true eternity—how then is it understood from the contrary when from the temporal to the intemporal some particular signification is transferred? They come, then, from the basis of likeness. But it must be asked what is that mode of likeness. In fact we express priority in four modes: of them the first is said to be priority of time, the second priority of rank, the third priority of origin, the fourth priority of eternity. Of those the following examples are found: in time the flower comes before the fruit; in rank the fruit comes before the flower; the voice comes in origin before the word; God in eternity comes before the creature. In the mode, then, in which God comes before all things that he made, that is in eternity, in that mode precisely he knew in advance and predestined what he would make. From this it is deduced that such words are taken metaphorically from the first mode to the fourth, that is, from their basis in time to their basis in eternity.

---

76. Cf. Augustine, *De trinitate* IV, 1, 3; *De Genesi ad litteram* II, 6, 12.

CHAPTER TEN

When God Is Said to Know in Advance and to Predestine Sins or Death or the Punishments of Men or Angels, It Is to Be Understood from the Contrary

1. It remains to consider the topos which, as we said before, is called *entimema* by dialecticians and rhetoricians but by grammarians ΚΑΤ ΑΝΤΙΦΡΑCΙΝ (by antiphrasis), and which is of all modes of reasoning and verbal signs the noblest. It has been shown that foreknowledge and predestination, just as preparation and foresight and suchlike, are predicated metaphorically of God and can be used in a transferred sense on two bases of signification, and that they are correctly called relational because they are proved to come both from the basis of likeness and from the basis that is called 'from contrariety'. Here it is very clearly understood and most firmly held that in these words, when they are taken according to likeness, nothing else is meant except the fact that the creator of all things will act. And whether in creating the substance of the universe with its natural qualities or in administering it, this will only include those whom he foreknew and predestined, according to the disposition of his

grace, to be conformed to the image of his own son. But when those same words are transferred metaphorically from the basis that is in 'contrariety', nothing is to be understood in them except what God permitted to take place in the creature which he created, by the individual and free movement of a rational nature which perversely uses the natural good things received through the generosity of its creator. And that is the sum total of what is called evil and its various punishments and unhappiness of every kind.

2. Therefore when we hear it said that God foreknew or predestined or prepared sins or death or the punishments of those whom he justly abandoned, that is, whom he allowed each to be punished by his own personal perversity, we have to understand those expressions altogether 'from the contrary' so that the heretical distortion originating from the misuse of such words may not lead us astray. For they do not see the light of the inner eyes who care little for the fact that all evil proceeding from a perverse will, is nothing. Let me omit that class of evil things that is called evil by that same rule of contrariety, even if by nature it be good, that is to say that eternal fire which is prepared for the devil and his accomplices.[77] All other things that are properly called evil, originating from one cause—that is, as has often been said, the perverse movement of a will that is free and changeable turning itself away from the creator and misusing the creation—all these other things are summed up between two limits, one of which is sin, the other its punishment.[78]

3. All evil, then, is either sin or the punishment of sin. Regarding those two: if no true reasoning allows that God knows of them in advance, how all the more could anyone dare to say that he predestines them, except 'by contrariety'? Why! Surely we cannot rightly think of God—who alone is true essence,[79] who made all things that are to the extent that they are—as possessing foreknowledge or predestination of those things which are not himself and have not come from him because they are nothing? For if knowledge is nothing other than the understanding of the things that are, by what reasoning should there be said to be knowledge or foreknowledge in the case of things that are not? In the same way, if predestination is nothing other than the preparation of those things which

---

77. Cf. Augustine, *De natura boni* 38.38 (*The Nature of the Good* CC 6; CUA 88; NPN 4); *De ciuitate Dei* XII, 4 (*City of God*, numerous translations).
78. Cf. Augustine, *De uera religione* 12, 23.
79. Cf. Augustine, *De trinitate* VII, 5, 10.

God foresaw were to be made, how can predestination be asserted of those things which God neither made nor prepared to be made? Furthermore, if evil is nothing other than the corruption of good, and all good either is God and cannot be corrupted, or from God and can be corrupted, and all corruption seeks nothing else than that the good exist not, who can doubt that evil is that which strives to destroy good so that it may not exist? Evil, then, neither is God nor from God. And for this reason, just as God is not the author of evil, so has he not foreknowledge of evil nor does he predestine it.

But if anyone doubts that evil is nothing other than the corruption of good, let him see what Augustine says on this matter, writing *Against the Epistle of Manichaeus Entitled Fundamental:* "Learn that evil is not a substance, but just as in the body beauty may by a change in form lose something for the worse, or rather be diminished, and what before was called beautiful is now said to be ugly, and the body said to displease which before had pleased, so rightly in the mind the ornament of the will by which one lives conscientiously and justly is disfigured by a will changed for the worse, and thus sin affects the wretched soul which had gained happiness by the honour of a righteous will, without the addition or removal of any substance. Who could doubt that the totality of what is called evil is nothing other than corruption? Indeed, various kinds of evils can be called by various kinds of names; but it is corruption which is the evil of all things within which any evil can be observed. But the corruption of an instructed soul is called ignorance, the corruption of the prudent called imprudence, the corruption of the just injustice, the corruption of courage cowardice, the corruption of rest and tranquility greed or fear or sadness or ostentation. Secondly, in the ensouled body the corruption of health is pain and disease, the corruption of energy weariness, the corruption of rest toil. Then in the physical body itself the corruption of beauty is ugliness, the corruption of the upright is crookedness, the corruption of order perversity, the corruption of wholeness division or fracture or diminution. It would be lengthy and difficult to list by name all the corruptions of these things I have drawn attention to as well as innumerable others, since many that are referred to in the body can be named also in the soul and there are countless areas in which corruption may have its own special terminology."[80]

---

80. *Contra Epistulam quam uocant Fundamenti* 27, 29; 35, 39 (*Against the Epistle of Manichaeus Entitled Fundamental* E 5; NPN 4).

4. This being the case, is there anyone who cannot see, unless he is devoid of understanding, that the whole of what is called sin and its consequences, established in death and unhappiness, is nothing other than the corruptions of the perfect and happy life, with the result that each is in turn opposed to each, that is to perfection sin, to life death, to happiness unhappiness. The first named exist, the last named are entirely non-existent; the first named strive upwards after the one beginning of all things, the last named desert and the good things they corrupt hasten downwards to return to nothingness; the cause of the first is God, of the others none; the first are comprehended within the bounds of natural forms in the lack and privation of which the others are known by not knowing. For just as the cause of an evil will cannot be either found or known, so of all the defects that deservedly follow upon it neither the efficient cause nor the defects themselves can be known because they are nothing. On this point I think that the testimony of Saint Augustine should be brought forward, for he says in Book XII, *On the City of God*:[81] "Let no one seek the efficient cause of an evil will; for it is not efficient but a deficiency. For to abandon what supremely exists for what is lower in its degree of being is to begin to possess an evil will. Moreover to wish to discover the causes of these deficiencies since they are not efficient but deficient, is as if someone should wish to see darkness or to hear silence. Yet each is known to us, the former only through the eyes and the latter only through the ears, known however not in species but the privation of species. But let no one seek to know from me that of which I know I am ignorant, unless perhaps to learn not to know what must be known to be unknowable. In fact those things that are known not in species but in the privation thereof—if it is possible to say or understand this—are in a certain way known by not knowing, with the result that by knowing they are not known. For when the glance of the bodily eye runs through corporeal species it nowhere sees darkness except after it has begun not to see. Likewise it pertains to no other sense but to the ears alone to perceive silence, which nevertheless is perceived in no other way than by not hearing. Thus our mind by understanding perceives, indeed, the intelligible species, but when these are lacking it learns by not knowing. For who has an understanding of things that are lacking?"[82]

81. *De ciuitate Dei* XII, 7.
82. Cf. Ps. 18.13.

5. And so by these arguments it is firmly concluded that every defect of a perverse will—or deficiency or privation, or however one may describe that mortal movement by which the highest good is abandoned so that the spirit wanders off without returning—and the end of this, death in fact and the unhappiness of eternal punishments, are altogether nothing. For all that lacks matter, form and species is, without doubt, nothing: but it is clear that those three are missing in all absence of things and in all deficiency of them. Therefore absence and deficiency are completely non-existent. And on that account they can neither be foreknown nor predestined by him who supremely exists. How surprising or rather lamentable is the blindness of those who are unwilling to understand 'by contrariety', if ever they gather from divine or human authority that God has had foreknowledge of or has predestined sins, death, punishments, which are utterly nothing because they are deficiencies. For what is sin but the deficiency of justice? What is death but the deficiency of life? What is punishment but the deficiency of happiness? If those people considered more carefully that all the things that are are for no other reason than because they were foreknown and predestined, but all the things that are not 'are not' for no other reason than that they were neither foreknown nor predestined, perhaps they would correct themselves and become reasonable. They might turn their mind to the light of truth in order that in it and through it they might be able to perceive that whatever is truly found to exist in the whole universe is nothing other than the one true essence which everywhere is wholly in itself. And what is that but the prescient predestination of all natures and the predestining foreknowledge? But if it is quite clearly understood that there is no supreme and principal substance of all natures beyond the divine foreknowledge and predestination, how can it be believed to exist in those things which are utterly non-existent? For if it were in them, they would certainly have subsisted not as nothing but as something. But they are in fact nothing. In them, therefore, there is neither divine foreknowledge nor divine predestination.

CHAPTER ELEVEN

It Can Be Established by Divine and Human Authority That God's Predestination Concerns Only Those Who Are Prepared for Eternal Happiness

1. But since in our present deliberation the principal question posed is divine foreknowledge and predestination—and for a more thorough treatment of it incidental questions have necessarily been introduced—it should be somewhat more openly investigated in the light of examples. For our first concern has been to convince the readers of our writings, if indeed there should be any to have judged them worth reading. Our wish is that their charity would extend to examining them thoroughly, observing in them our dedication to obedience rather than despising the usefulness of our slight argument, if there be any usefulness in it. And if they are, perhaps, in some way provoked, they should not attack us, saying that we are suppressors of both divine foreknowledge and divine predestination, because if they are more careful in their scrutiny, they will find in the arguments a great deal of affirmation but nothing of suppression.

TREATISE ON DIVINE PREDESTINATION

What then? Does one really either undermine the foreknowledge of God or devalue his predestination by stating that they are predicated of God metaphorically? As if a transference could not be made from temporal things to eternal by some mode of similitude, or from the things which are to the things which are not, by the most beauteous mode of contrariety? Or as if one were opposing the true faith in saying that foreknowledge and predestination are properly in the things which in order of time precede the things which they both foreknow and predestine, but that foreknowledge and predestination are improper terms in the case of him to whom there are no things in the future, since not in any time but in his own eternity he precedes all things that are from him? Or how is it inconsisent with the truth if one says in the mode of similitude: 'God foreknew all that he was going to do,' and that it be said in the mode of contrariety: 'He foreknew what he was not going to do,' instead of 'he did not know'? Likewise concerning predestination, it should be understood by similitude: 'God predestined those whom he prepared for receiving his freely-given grace'; and by contrariety: 'He predestined the wicked to death, or eternal punishment,' when nevertheless he did not predestine them. For if they are predestined, necessarily they will perish and will suffer unavoidable punishments. If that is so, how shall the world be justly judged if the necessity of predestination drives it to perdition? That opinion is to be considered characteristic of the ungodly.

2. Accordingly, lest this exercise of our reasoning powers appear to be supported by no principle of divine or human authority, we must investigate what can be effected by the pages of divine scripture, what by the words of the holy father Augustine; not because we cannot reach these same conclusions by examples of other catholic fathers, but because we think it necessary and see it as useful and relevant to cite the words of that author to whom the heretic Gottschalk is principally accustomed to refer the causes of his abominable doctrine. For in truth there is no passage of scripture from which those who do not understand it cannot easily think up perversities. Hence it is that the forementioned lying adulterator of the holy fathers deservedly—if only because he is neither an investigator nor a discoverer of the truth—did not understand what that father Augustine wished to make known by his words but, in order to advocate what he himself by his own and the devil's agency invented, in fact violently twisted the words of the forementioned father out of all consistency and clearly in self-contradiction.

God's Predestination Concerns Only Those Who Are Prepared

3. Here in the first place it is to be noted that the firm authority of holy scripture is found to have established foreknowledge at the same time as predestination, or predestination alone absolutely, only in those whom God chose for the possession of eternal happiness. To prove this the words of the apostle suffice. For, speaking to the Romans,[83] he says: "We know that for those who love God all things are made to collaborate towards good, for those who are called according to what was proposed; because those whom he knew in advance he also predestined to come to share in the likeness of his own son, that he may be the firstborn among many brothers; but those whom he predestined he also called; and those whom he called he also justified; but those whom he justified he also glorified." Also to the Ephesians:[84] "Blessed be God and the Father of our lord Jesus Christ, who has blessed us in all spiritual benediction in the heavens in Christ Jesus. So too he has chosen us in himself before the creation of the world, that we might be holy and without stain in the sight of him in charity, predestining us for adoption as sons through Jesus Christ to himself, according to the pleasure of his will, for the praise of his glorious grace in which he has favoured us in his beloved son. In him we have redemption through his blood and remission of sins, according to the riches of his grace which he has poured out abundantly on us in all wisdom and prudence. And he has manifested to us the mystery of his will in accordance with his pleasure, which he proposed in Christ, to be carried out in the fullness of times, to restore in Christ all things that are in the heavens and upon the earth, in him whom also we are called by lot. For we are predestined according to God's purpose by him who arranges all things according to the design of his own will." Against such a clear trumpet-blast of truth as this, what man of prudent and watchful faith would give a hearing to human words? Who would not hear in it that predestination is in every way for the holy and is utterly impossible for the wicked?

4. The holy father Aurelius Augustine was indeed a most prolific author of christian eloquence, a most skilled investigator of the truth, and a most noble instructor in the literal and transferred use of language for the improvement of those who were going to read him. Yet at different times in the course of his writings he is found to have said that God predestined

---

83. Rom. 8.28–30; cf. Augustine, *De correptione et gratia* 9, 23 (*Rebuke/Admonition and Grace* E 15; FC 2; NPN 5).
84. Eph. 1.3–11; cf. Augustine, *De praedestinatione sanctorum* 18, 35 (E 15; NPN 5).

TREATISE ON DIVINE PREDESTINATION

the wicked to perdition or punishments, and for this reason he has become, as the apostle says,[85] for those who understand him, "an odour of life leading to life" but for those who do not understand, "an odour of death leading to death." Hence the reasoning of the present case requires that we cite his own words as if in contradiction of himself, so that the discerning reader may more easily direct his attention to the kind of language in which he said that divine predestination is appropriate for both classes of men, namely for the elect through grace, and for the abandoned through justice. We have judged, therefore, that those same words, by the misuse of which the heretic tries to support his perfidious error, should be cited in order that he retreat, wounded by those same arrows which he had recklessly twisted into the hearts of the simple.

5. Augustine says, then, in a homily[86] to the people expounding the passage of the Gospel: "'The prince of this world is already judged,'[87] that is, he is irrevocably destined for the judgment of eternal fire." Also in the exposition of the Gospel according to John,[88] where he is explaining the testimony of the precursor concerning Christ, he says: "Some people, prepared for the wrath of God, are to be damned by the devil"; also of the Jews: "These people are disdainful of death and are predestined to eternal death." "Also why did he say to the Jews: 'You do not believe because you are not from among my sheep,' unless because he saw them predestined to eternal destruction?" "Repeatedly what the lord says: 'No one can snatch from the hand of my Father,'" he follows with an explanation saying: "What can the wolf do, what the thief and the robber? They destroy only those predestined to destruction." In that book which he calls *Enchiridion*[89] (the manual of faith, hope and charity) he says: "These are the great works of the lord sought out in accordance with all his wills[90] and so wisely sought out that when the angelic and human creation had sinned, that is, had done not what he but what it willed, even through the same will of that creature by which there was done what the creator did not will, he would himself carry out what he did will. He would make good

---

85. Cf. 2 Cor. 2.16.
86. Augustine, *In Iohannis euangelium tractatus* 95, 4 (*Homilies on St. John's Gospel* E 10, 11; FC 78, 79; NPN 7).
87. John 16.11.
88. *Op. cit.*, 14, 8; 43,13; 48,4, 6; and cf. John 3.32; 10.26; 10.29.
89. Augustine, *Enchiridion ad Laurentium* 26, 100.
90. Cf. Ps. 111.2.

God's Predestination Concerns Only Those Who Are Prepared

use also of evil things, although he was supremely good, for the damnation of those whom he justly predestined to punishment and the salvation of those whom he bounteously predestined to grace." Also from that same book:[91] "The sons of hell also are said not to be born of it but to have been prepared for it, just as the sons of the kingdom are being prepared for the kingdom." In the book on *Man's Perfection in Righteousness*[92] he uses the expression: "In that class of men which is predestined for destruction." In the books of the *City of God*:[93] "What will he give to those whom he has predestined for life who has given such things as these to those whom he has predestined for death?"

6. By these and similar words of that catholic author the heretical madness raves and with wolfish teeth lacerates the faith of the less instructed. Who indeed, among those not familiar with the turns of speech which the holy fathers tend to use, could not be easily led astray by hearing of those predestined to eternal fire, prepared for the wrath of God, predestined to eternal death, predestined to destruction, to punishment, and to other things of that kind? He would concede without any hesitation either two predestinations, one plainly of the holy, the other of the unholy, altogether mutually contradictory: or he would say that one and the same divine predestination embraces both the holy and the unholy and is at the same time capable of contradictions. This reason rejects. Help is usefully at hand for his lamentably unhappy condition when that same predestination is defined according to the same Augustine, and his definition is defended by his own pleading. Be prepared, then, heretic, either to defend yourself, which you are in no way able to do, or to correct yourself, which you *are* able to do, if you would desist from opposing the truth. Listen to the terms of the definition of divine predestination, which no right believer dares either to lessen by curtailment or increase by extending, and which no contentious person can weaken. In the book addressed to Prosper and Hilary,[94] he says: "Predestination is that which without foreknowledge cannot be. But there can be foreknowledge without predestination. For by foreknowledge God knew beforehand those things which he had been going to do; hence it has been said: 'He has made the things

---

91. *I.e.* Augustine, *Enchiridion* 12, 39.
92. *Id., De perfectione iustitiae hominis* 13, 31 (*Man's Perfection in Righteousness* E 4, NPN 5).
93. *Id., De ciuitate Dei* XXII, 24, 5.
94. *Id., De praedestinatione sanctorum* 10, 19.

that are going to be.'⁹⁵ But he can know beforehand even those things he does not himself do, such as whatever sins are committed."

7. Take note how this definition is of the kind that is obtained from distinction of species from genus. There is, then, such a difference between predestination and foreknowledge that all predestination is foreknowledge but not all foreknowledge is predestination. For the very foreknowledge by which God has known in advance the things which he himself had been going to make is truly and specifically called predestination. But that foreknowledge by which he has known in advance the things he does not make, that is sins and their punishment, is by agreement absolutely called foreknowledge, in such a way that only that foreknowledge which is called predestination is always understood in a good sense; but foreknowledge alone without predestination is of wholly bad things which God does not make. And lest anyone had any doubt about that, Augustine added: "Therefore the predestination of God in the good man is the preparation of grace; but grace is the effect of predestination itself." Also in the book *On the Gift of Perseverance*⁹⁶ he more clearly demonstrates the same matters: "On whomsoever, therefore, God bestows those gifts of his, he has beyond doubt foreknown that he will bestow them, and in his foreknowledge prepared them. Those, then, whom he predestined, he called also by that call of which it was said: 'Without change of heart are God's gifts and his call.'⁹⁷ For indeed the disposition of his future works in his foreknowledge, which cannot be mistaken or changed, is entirely predestination, and nothing other than it." To this most clear and manifest trumpet-blast of the christian camp who would presume to sound a discordant note? It does not cease to re-echo the words that for God to predestine is nothing other than to dispose by his foreknowledge the works which he was going to do. Tell me, please, whether this definition of predestination is true or false. If it is false, take Augustine to task; if it is true, action must be taken, as he says in the book *On the Greatness of the Soul*:⁹⁸ "The definition contains nothing less, nothing more than what was undertaken to be explained; otherwise it would be utterly defective." But whether it is free of faults of this kind is now being examined by the method of conversion.

95. Isa. 45.11.
96. Augustine, *De dono perseuerantiae* 17, 41.
97. Rom. 8.30; 11.29.
98. Augustine, *De quantitate animae* 25, 47 (*The Greatness/Magnitude of the Soul* ACW 9; FC 4).

CHAPTER TWELVE

The Definition of Predestination

1. The conversion of this definition should, then, be as follows. If it is true that by one's foreknowledge, which cannot be mistaken or changed, one disposes one's future works, and absolutely that and nothing else is to predestine; then it is true also that to predestine is absolutely and nothing other than in one's foreknowledge, which cannot be mistaken or changed, to dispose one's future works. From this another conversion is inferred. If all foreknowledge by which God disposed his future works is divine predestination, all predestination by which God disposed his future works is divine foreknowledge; it follows then that the predestination of God does not exist except in his works, since nothing less and nothing more is contained in its definition beyond the disposition of God's works.

2. But in response to these remarks you will say that it justly pertains to the works of God to predestine for punishment those who are to be damned, just as it pertains to his works to predestine to happiness those who are to be saved by grace—and you will attempt to confirm this by the evidence of the same saint Augustine.[99] I have cited those words in the order in which you have cited them, so that we may see in them not what you but what he intended. If one passage among them is expounded correctly, it will suffice for the understanding of the others. Let us then

---

99. Cf. chap. 11 above, pars. 5, 7 and notes.

cite that one: "'Great are the works of the lord sought out in accordance with all his wills,' and so wisely sought out that when the angelic and human creature had sinned, that is, had done not what he but what it willed, even by means of the same will of that creature, by which there was done what the creator did not will, he would himself carry out what he did will, making good use also of evil things although he was supremely good, for the damnation of those whom he justly predestined to punishment and the salvation of those whom he bounteously predestined to grace." Note that in one and the same sentence he says: "He predestined to punishment," "he predestined to grace." What, we ask, are you to reply to our questions as to whether it pertains to the justice of God or to his grace to predestine the ungodly to punishment? You will reply, I believe, to justice: for he says "those whom justly he predestined to punishment," not therefore to grace. And for this reason, if the predestination of punishment is not a gift of God but the judgment of sin, it necessarily follows either that Augustine's own statement that "the predestination of God which is in the good is the preparation of grace" is false or, from 'contrariety', the predestination of punishments will be accepted. But what he has said is true and immutable: "the predestination of God which is in the good is the preparation of grace." It was from 'contrariety', then, that he wished his proposition, "he predestined to punishment" to be understood.

3. But in case you should raise the objection that he did not say: "the predestination of God is the preparation of grace," but: "the predestination of God which is in the good is the preparation of grace," where room seems to be left for another predestination which is, as it were, in the bad; or it is not said to be impossible that the same predestination, if it is the single and only one, occurs in the good and bad; take note first that one definition cannot at all contain two predestinations. Secondly, if no other more true or more fitting definition of predestination were to be found than the one mentioned above, and it includes nothing except the divine works which are good, as no faithful believer doubts, what obliges us to understand any other ulterior meaning when we hear "the predestination of God which is in the good," except that it is always both good and in the good?

4. But if you say that to predestine the ungodly to punishment is good and thus to be considered among the works of God, we reply: "good because just." But because it is not the gift of God, since it is his judgment, and every predestination of God is completely the preparation of

Definition of Predestination

grace and every grace a gift, all divine predestination is necessarily concluded to be the preparation of his gifts. Doubtless, punishment justly torments the ungodly, and that is not a gift; otherwise, if it were a gift, it would not torment but would certainly liberate. There is not, then, a predestination to punishment. If there were, it would not be punishment but grace. But it is punishment. There is not, therefore, predestination to it.

Accordingly, if anyone still doubts that predestination is always to be understood within the gifts of divine bounty, he should examine attentively the book of Saint Augustine, *On the Gift of Perseverance*[100] in that passage where he says: "The gifts, I say, of God, if there is no predestination, such as we are maintaining, are not foreknown by God. But they are foreknown. This is, then, the predestination that we are maintaining. Hence the same predestination is sometimes indicated also by the name of foreknowledge, as the apostle says: 'God did not repudiate his people whom he knew beforehand.'[101] This 'knew beforehand' that he speaks of is not correctly understood except as 'predestine', as the context of the passage itself shows. For he was speaking about the remnant of the Jews which had been saved, while the rest perished. For he had said earlier that the prophet had said to Israel: 'All day I have stretched out my hands to an unbelieving and rebellious people.'[102] And as if the answer had been: 'Where then are the promises made by God to Israel?' he had immediately added: 'I say then, surely God has not repudiated his own people? God forbid; for I too am an Israelite of the seed of Abraham, of the tribe of Benjamin':[103] as if he said: 'for I too am one of the people'. Then he added the words we are now discussing: 'God did not repudiate his own people whom he knew beforehand.' And in order to show that the remnant had been left by God's grace, not by the merits of their own works, he added as well: 'Do you not know what the scripture says of Elias, how he interceded with God against Israel' and so on. 'But what,' he asks, 'does God's answer tell him? "I have left for myself seven thousand men who have not bent the knee before Baal."' For he does not say: 'there are left to me,' or 'they have left themselves to me,' but: 'I have left for myself.' 'So then,' he says, 'in this present time also a remnant is formed by the election of

---

100. Augustine, *De dono perseuerantiae* 17, 47-19, 49.
101. Rom. 11.2.
102. Rom. 10.21; Isa. 65, 2.
103. The Augustinian passage is commenting on Rom. 11.1-7 and, in turn, on the Pauline references to 1 (3) Kings 19.10, 18.

grace. But if by grace, then no longer by works; otherwise grace is no longer grace.' And connecting those words with what I have already cited above. 'What then?' he asks. And in reply to this enquiry: 'Israel did not gain what it was seeking, but the chosen did, and the rest were blinded.' In those chosen, therefore, and in this remnant which was made by the election of grace, he intended to be understood the people whom God did not repudiate because he knew them beforehand. This is that election by which he chose those whom he willed in Christ before the foundation of the world, that they might be holy and unspotted in the sight of him in love, predestining them for adoption as sons.[104] No one, then, who understands this is permitted to deny or to doubt that, when the apostle says: 'God did not repudiate his people whom he knew beforehand,' he wished to signify predestination. For he knew beforehand the remnant which he was going to form according to the election of grace, that is to say, therefore, the remnant which he had predestined: for certainly he knew it in advance if he predestined it. But to have predestined is to have known beforehand what he was going to do.

"What prevents us, therefore, from understanding the same predestination when we read of God's foreknowledge in some commentators on the word of God, and the discussion is on the calling of the elect? For in that matter they preferred, perhaps, to use this word which, as well as being more easily understood, is not inconsistent with, but in fact is in accordance with, the truth which is asserted concerning the predestination to grace. This I know, that no one has been able to argue except in error against that predestination which I am defending in accordance with the holy scriptures."

5. If, therefore, we are to yield to the authority of Saint Augustine, or rather through it to the truth, we must unshakeably hold to this rule, that whenever we find divine foreknowledge either in holy scripture or in its commentators, if the discussion has been about the election of the holy, we are to take it to mean nothing else at all except predestination. And if that is so, who cannot see that all God's foreknowledge relating to the saints is nothing other than their predestination? Accordingly, by the links of true reasoning it can be concluded as follows: all foreknowledge relating to the elect is predestination; there is no predestination except of the elect; therefore no foreknowledge relating to the elect is not predesti-

---

104. Eph. 1.4.

Definition of Predestination

nation. No one is elected to punishment. How, then is the punishment predestined that is proper to the wicked? Is it perhaps that, just as some are called elect who have not been chosen, so also by writers people are often called predestined who have not been predestined, children of God who are not his children, in that mode of contrariety earlier mentioned?

6. But if you are looking for where the wicked are found to be called elect, even though they have not been chosen, and called children of God, who are not his children, study Saint Augustine in the book to Prosper and Hilary,[105] where he speaks in words to this effect: "Whoever are chosen are also, without doubt, called, but not all who are called are as a consequence chosen. Those, therefore, are chosen, as has often been said, who are called according to plan, who are also predestined and known beforehand. If any of these perishes, God is in error; but none of them perishes, because God is not in error. If any of them perishes, it is by human failure that God is overcome; but none of them perishes, because God is overcome by nothing. For they are chosen to reign with Christ, not as Judas was chosen for the work to which he was suited; for he was chosen by him who knows how to make good use even of the bad, so that also, through that damnable act of his, that venerable deed might be accomplished for which Christ had come. Therefore, when we hear: 'Did I not choose you twelve, and one of you is a devil'[106] ought we not to understand that they were chosen by mercy, Judas by judgment, they to obtain the kingdom, Christ to shed his blood? 'But the foundation of God stands firm, having this as its seal: God knew who are his.'[107] Their faith, which indeed works by love,[108] either does not at all fail, or if there are some in whom it fails, it is restored before this life comes to an end and, when the offending iniquity is wiped out, perseverance to the end is allotted to them. But as to those who are not going to persevere, and who will fall away from christian faith and conduct, so that the end of this life will find them in that same state, there is no doubt that, even at the time when they are living good and pious lives, they are not to be reckoned among those who persevere. For they are not set apart from that mass of perdition by the foreknowledge of God and

---

105. Eriugena appears here to have confused his reference which is, in fact, to *De correptione et gratia*, 7, 14, 16; 9, 20; works addressed to Prosper and Hilary were *De praedestinatione sanctorum* and *De dono perseuerantiae*.
106. John 6.70.
107. 2 Tim. 2.19.
108. Gal. 5.6.

predestination. And so neither are they called according to plan, and for this reason they are not chosen, but are 'called' among those of whom it was said: 'Many are called but few are chosen.'[109] And yet who would deny that they are chosen, when they believe and are baptized and live according to God? Nevertheless they are called elect by those who do not know what they will be, not by him who knows that they have not the perseverance which leads the elect to the blessed life, and who knows that they stand now, just as he will have known beforehand that they will fall. And it should not disturb us that to some of his children God does not give this perseverance. God forbid that it should be so if these were from among those predestined and called according to plan. But they are not the children of the promise—for those, when they live good lives, are called the children of God—but because they will live wickedly and die in the same wickedness, God's foreknowledge does not call them children of God. For there are children of God who are not yet such for us but are already such for God. Of these John the evangelist says that 'Jesus was to die for the people and not only for the people, but to gather into one the children of God who were scattered.'[110] Children of God certainly they were going to be, by believing through the preaching of the gospel, and yet before this had happened they were already children of God, firmly and immovably enrolled in the remembrance-book of their father. And again there are some called by us children of God because of grace received even for a time, and they are not so called by God. Of them the same John says: 'They went out from us, but they were not of us.'[111] Therefore, when the words 'the children of God' are said of those who did not have perseverance, 'who went from us but were not of us,' and there is also added: 'because if they had been of us, they would certainly have stayed with us,' what else is said of them but that they were not children, even when they professed to be and were called children?"

---

109. Matt. 20.16.
110. John 11.51–52.
111. 1 John 2.19. Here Eriugena omits a portion of Augustine's text and slightly adapts the concluding portion.

CHAPTER THIRTEEN

What Can Be Inferred from the above Judgment of Saint Augustine

1. If the words of that judgment are a little more carefully considered, they are sufficient to prove what we are attempting to advocate. And so, taking up what the lord said to his disciples: "Did I not choose you twelve, and one of you is a devil,"[112] he added that we must understand that they, that is, the apostles, eleven then in number, were called according to the purpose of grace; he, namely the betrayer, was called by judgment, and rejected according to the balancing of justice. They were chosen for glory, he for punishment; in them were to be understood all those to be saved by grace who would abide in goodness to the end of this life; in him all who were to die by judgment were included. Called at the proper time, soon to abandon the purpose of godly living, they are all, nevertheless, said to be chosen, although they are not chosen unless they share the image of the son of God. But others are regarded as chosen by those ignorant of what they will be; and in this way they are not elected but rejected. They are said to be children of God although they are sons of perdition, all of whom the lord designated in his own betrayer. For, praying to his father on behalf of his own chosen ones, he said: "Those whom

---

112. John 6.70.

you gave me I have guarded, and none of them has perished except the son of perdition."[113] Judas, then, was said to be chosen because he was called among the chosen ones; he was said to be a son because he was numbered among the brothers of Christ by those who were in ignorance. But just as no one disputes that it is 'by contrariety' that any are called children other than those for whom the paternal inheritance is determined, so in the same way no one disputes that it is 'by contrariety' that any are elect except those set apart for the joy of blessedness within that community of those others whom the 'mass of the damned' justly confines in misery. And just as they are not children if not heirs, so they are not elect if they are not beloved. How, therefore, unless 'by contrariety', could Judas be said to be elect if he was not beloved? For if he were beloved he certainly would not be rejected? Or how could he be chosen for the judgment of eternal fire who, if he had been chosen, would without doubt attain eternal life?

2. But if these arguments are shamelessly resisted, the improper use of the term 'election' of Judas we must understand by his just rejection, and by his sonship,[114] through which at the appointed time he was called, his just and deservedly eternal repudiation. For he was never chosen, just as at no time was he not rejected, like a friend who was always an enemy. Accordingly I do not see why the holy fathers would hesitate, with a fine turn of phrase, to speak out confidently about those predestined to punishment or death or other things of that sort, whenever they decided to consider the matter in the course of their writings, since they did not doubt that truth itself had spoken in that same fashion. Neither would they have abandoned the traces of the highest wisdom which was speaking in them, and they would have adorned their own eloquence with the most precious gems of figurative expression to provide an example to future readers. If, therefore, the lord was not embarrassed to refer to his betrayer as chosen, why should his imitator, Saint Augustine, blush to call the same man, that is the betrayer, predestined? And likewise, why would he hesitate to say that the Jewish people, filled with envious perfidy, the betrayers of our lord Jesus Christ and in this way his slayers, were predestined to destruction? Furthermore, why should not all the wicked in general be declared to be predestined to torment, when the most valid reasoning advocates and the clearest authority confirms that there are no

113. *Ibid.* 17.12.
114. Eriugena's term is *filiolitas*.

children of God apart from his chosen, and none of his chosen except those predestined by him; and conversely, there are none predestined but those chosen, nor any chosen except his children.

3. Hence by an irreversible conclusion it follows that if all the children of God are chosen—and it is impious to deny it—but all those chosen are beyond doubt predestined, therefore all the children of God are predestined. This conclusion is not vitiated by 'conversion', and in no way wavers: if all those predestined are chosen—as none of the faithful doubts—but all the chosen are certainly the children of God, then all who are predestined are the children of God. This conclusion could by no means stand if the three terms were not equal, that is sonship, election and predestination. For, all that is included in sonship is also included in election, and in election all that is in predestination. And thus the three equal terms unfailingly occur and recur. Therefore, just as the children of God are sought in vain outside of his elect, in the same way it is pointless to think of his elect outside of those predestined by him. And reciprocally: just as it is wicked to consider that there are some predestined by God apart from his elect, so it is superfluous to think that there are any elect of God apart from his children. Therefore, they are not predestined if they are not to be children of God. For as it is not possible that at the same time the children of God should be both chosen and not predestined, so it is impossible that at the same time they should be both predestined and not the chosen children of God. Accordingly, who can explain the description of the perfidious Jews to whom the saviour said: "You are from the devil your father,"[115] as *predestined* by God to destruction, when everyone predestined by God must be his chosen, and for that reason his child, unless one considers that 'basis of opposites', which we have often repeated, from which such a form of statement is taken 'by contrariety'?

4. Down then with the garrulous impudence of the heretics. Let the sound faith of the predestined, the chosen, the children of God hold this rule unshaken, that whenever they hear or read of persons as predestined to evil, to punishment, to destruction or torment, they are to understand nothing other than that they have not been predestined, but that they have not been separated from the mass of those damnable by the deserts of original sin and their own sin, and thus allowed to live wickedly, abandoned, to be punished afterwards with eternal fire.

---

115. John 8.44.

CHAPTER FOURTEEN

Collected Attestations of Saint Augustine by Which It Is Clearly Proved That There Is but One Predestination and It Refers Only to the Saints

1. And lest anyone think, perhaps, that we have made such statements on the basis of our own personal understanding unsupported by the weight of any authority, we have decided to bring together the attestations of the holy father Augustine, so that every intelligent person should know that he in no way taught two predestinations, neither a single bipartite one, nor a double one, as Gottschalk informs us, and that that single one, namely the divine one, pertains only to the saints but can in no way be of the wicked. In the treatise *On Rebuke and Grace*[116] he says: "To the saints predestined for the kingdom of God by the grace of God the gift of perseverance is given, not only so that they cannot without that gift continue persevering, but also so that by means of the gift they cannot but

---

116. Augustine, *De correptione et gratia* 12, 34, 36.

continue persevering." And somewhat further on: "He therefore makes them to persevere in good who has made them good; but those who fall and perish were not in the number of the predestined." Take note how absolutely he said: "those who fall and perish were not in the number of the predestined." How would he say these things if he wished to defend either two predestinations, or one divided in two parts, or double, one indeed of the saints but the other allotted to the wicked? For if there were two, there would necessarily be one apportioned to those to whom is given the gift of perseverance, the other to those falling and perishing, to whom it is not given; yet no man would be excluded from the number of the predestined. For if he were expelled from the number of the predestined who live by standing firm, he would be accepted among the number of those predestined who perish by falling. Likewise, if one was divided in two parts, or double, necessarily it would include in one of its parts those lost, in the other those freed. Who then among men or angels, good or bad, may not be in the number of the predestined? Or does the heretic, perhaps, point to a third class both of men and angels which, because it is neither good nor bad, goes outside the number of the predestined? If this is quite erroneous, it remains that there are only two classes both of men and of angels. For reason makes this distinction: every man is either good or bad; so also for the angel.

2. If predestination, therefore, as has been said, were divided into two species or parts, of which one included the good, the other the bad, who could be found outside the number of those predestined? And if it were so, how could the forementioned author declare: "those who fall and perish were not in the number of the predestined"? For he does not say: "they were not in the number of those predestined to life," but in absolute terms: "they were not in the number of those predestined." If, therefore, they were not in the number of those predestined, they were outside that number. By this it is proved that those falling and perishing were not in any way predestined. This is demonstrated very clearly in the words that follow, where he says:[117] "Lest fearful infections spread slowly through many of them, pastoral necessity has to remove the diseased animal from the healthy sheep, to be cured perhaps in that very separation by him to whom nothing is impossible. For we, who do not know who belongs to the number of the predestined and who does not belong, should be so affected by compassion and love that we wish all to be saved. Consequently, as far

---

117. Augustine, *De correptione et gratia* 15, 46; 16, 49.

as in us lies, because we are unable to distinguish those predestined from those not predestined, we ought to wish all to be saved; and, so that they may not perish or bring others to ruin, we must by way of remedy issue a severe rebuke to all. But it is God's part to make that rebuke beneficial for them, because he has known beforehand and predestined them to be conformed to the image of his son."

3. Here there is given us to understand the bipartite division of the entire rational creation into those who are, certainly, in the number of the predestined and those who are outside the number of the predestined. "For not knowing," he says, "who belongs to the number of the predestined, who does not belong." And again: "We who are unable to distinguish the predestined from those [not] predestined." From this is constructed a fourfold inquiry into truth by means of a tetragon: every man is either just or unjust. Again: every man is either predestined or not predestined. If it is true that every just man is predestined, it is false that every just man is not predestined. Again, if it is true that every unjust man is not predestined, it is false that every unjust man is predestined. Observe the force of the reasoning: two universal affirmatives correspond with one another. For, even as every just man is predestined, so every predestined man is just. In the same way two universal negatives agree with one another. For, in the manner in which every unjust man is not predestined, so every man not predestined is unjust. Again, to use the words of Augustine himself, every man either belongs or does not belong to the number of the predestined. But who among the wise doubts that of all men there are two classes, since truth proclaims without obscurity that there are only two ends of mankind, one indeed consisting of those allocated to eternal torment, but the other of those enjoying eternal life? Therefore the two are mutually opposed, eternal life and eternal torment. Accordingly the end of those belonging to the number of the predestined is eternal life, but the end of those not belonging to the number of the predestined is eternal torment.

But because we promised to bring together the attestations of Saint Augustine, it was decided to bring up only those in which, more clearly than light, divine predestination is stated to pertain only to the preparation of the gifts of God which he will bestow upon his elect and for that reason to have no reference at all to what does not pertain to his greatest gifts of mercy but to his most just and secret judgments. Nevertheless, as often said, authors are found who by means of that common figure of speech *antiphrasis* (the antiphrase) declare some predestined to punishments.

In the treatise *On the Gift of Perseverance*[118] he says: "Of two babies, equally bound by original sin, why one is adopted, the other one abandoned, and of two wicked men already of mature age, why one is called in such a way that he follows the caller, but the other either is not called, or is not called in that way, such are the inscrutable judgments of God. But why one of two pious men should be given perseverance to the end, the other not given it, are even more inscrutable judgments of God. Yet to the faithful this must be certain: that the former was from among those predestined, the latter was not." In the same treatise: "Will anyone dare to say that God did not know in advance those to whom he would give the capacity to believe, or those whom he would give to his son, so that from them he would not lose anyone? Undoubtedly, if he did foreknow these things, he certainly foreknew his own favours by which he deigns to set us free. This is the predestination of the saints and nothing else, namely the foreknowledge and preparation of the favours of God by which all who are set free are most surely set free. Where then are the others left by the just divine judge but in the mass of perdition, where the inhabitants of Tyre and Sidon were left, who could also have believed if they had seen the signs given by Christ? But because it was not given to them to believe, the means of belief were also denied them. From which it appears that some have, by nature, in their own character, the divine gift of understanding by which they are moved to faith if they either hear words or see signs in harmony with their minds, and to whom nevertheless, if by the higher judgment of God they are not set apart by the predestination of grace from the mass of perdition, neither those same divine words nor divine deeds are made available by which they would be able to believe." And a little before the end of the same treatise: "There is, I say, no more illustrious example of predestination than the mediator himself. Any believer who wishes to understand the matter well, let him pay attention to him, and in him he will also find himself," most clearly concluding that all the predestined are in Christ, and outside of him is no predestined person.

4. That God, however, predestined nobody to punishment but did prepare, that is predestined, punishment for those to be deservedly damned, is very clearly demonstrated by words of his, such as these. For he says[119] that "a just and merciful God, who knows future things in ad-

---

118. *De dono perseuerantiae* 9, 21; 14, 35; 24, 67.
119. PseudoAugustine, *Hypomnesticon* VI, 2, 2; 5, 7; 6, 8. (*PL* 45 and ed. J. Chisholm, Fribourg, Switzerland, 1980).

vance, out of this damnable mass, not by 'acceptance of persons,' but by the irreproachable judgment of his equity, prepares by his freely-given mercy those whom he knows beforehand, that is, he predestines them to eternal life, while the others, as I have said before, he punishes with the suffering they have earned. Those whom he punishes in this way, because he foreknew what they would be, he did not himself, however, make or predestine for punishing, but only, as I have said, foreknew within the damnable mass. For we have said, concerning the damnable mass of mankind that God foreknew those whom by his mercy, not by their deserts, he predestined to life by the grace of his election; but the others, who in the judgment of his justice were made destitute of grace, he had only foreknown that they would perish by their own fault, and had not predestined that they would perish. For those, however, who are either unwilling to accept the faith of salvation as preached to them, or in God's judgment are unable to, or having accepted it, misuse it, and for this reason are 'given over to depraved thoughts to practise what is not decent,'[120] we acknowledge that punishment has properly been predestined. Therefore we must hold to the rule of this unshaken reasoning, a rule become luminous by divine testimonies, namely, that sinners in their own wickedness are in the world foreknown only, not predestined; but that punishment is predestined because of the fact that they are foreknown.

5. By these and similar utterances of our most holy father Augustine it is easy enough, in my opinion, to convince pious believers of what true reason recommends, namely that God in no way predestined sinners for punishment, but that by their own deserts condign punishments have been predestined for them by him. This we can conjecture even from human laws. For, no temporal laws determine a man to sin; but by determining punishments for those who will sin they are seen to seek nothing else than to restrain, in fear of the harshness of the punishments, those who are prone to sin, and in this way to treat their offenders with no less mercy than punishment. For never has a state decreed that men should sin; but it has decreed that criminals be corrected by just punishment. And if this is so with laws that are transitory due to temporal mutability, how should one consider it to be with the eternal laws filled with the immutable strength of piety and justice?

---

120. Cf. Rom. 1.28.

CHAPTER FIFTEEN

By What Kind of Expressions God Is Said to Have Foreknowledge of Sins since They Are Nothing, or to Predestine the Punishments of Them Which Likewise Are Nothing

1. There is need, however, for greater consideration of what divine and human teaching most often impresses on us, namely that God foreknows the forbidden sins of his creatures and predestines the just punishments of them. For reason does not hesitate to proclaim that sins and their punishments are nothing, and hence they cannot be either foreknown or predestined. For, are things which do not exist either foreknown or predestined? I am of the opinion, therefore, that we need to establish by what figurative modes of speech such arguments can be brought forward. In fact, I think, insofar as I could prove it, I did in earlier discussions make clear, and confirmed by example of similes, that whenever we can find such a form of expression, as we often read, particularly in the treatises of Saint Augustine, namely that God predestined the wicked to sins and to the merited punishment of them, our best way of understanding it was by the mode of contrariety, as has often been said.

2. Of this form the most obvious example is found in the most impious betrayer of our lord. For by that same mode of speech that same man is said to be predestined who was chosen by the lord. Here we ought rightly to understand by 'chosen', not chosen but deservedly ignored for his perfidy and driven out; and by that same person being 'predestined' nothing other than not predestined, abandoned in the chaos of wrath, deprived of the gift of grace, an enemy, not a friend. And yet out of the mouth of him whom he betrayed he heard: "Friend, to what purpose have you come?"[121] Also elsewhere, as if as a sharer in divine love gathered among the truly predestined chosen friends, he had heard in a figurative mode: "I do not call you servants but friends."[122] In a similar way, although he had abdicated all heavenly paternity to him, as to a child among children the lord said: "Do not call any father on earth yours, for yours is one father who is in heaven."[123] And it is as if the gift of understanding seems to be bestowed on a wise man among wise men when it is said to the apostles: "To you it is given to know the mysteries of the kingdom."[124] If these and such things are to be understood 'by contrariety' about an impious man, why wonder that both he and the partners of his wickedness should by the same right be called predestined? For just as none of the wicked is elected to glory, so none of them is predestined to punishment. For just as election in no way exceeds the number of the predestined, so predestination in no way exceeds the number of the elect.

3. This same kind of expression, by which God is said to have predestined the unjust to punishments or to their sins, would seem to be rightly understood as though it were said that God had foreknown that the unjust would be sinners and would undergo punishments. Therefore, just as knowledge always, when the elect are in question, is rightly understood instead of predestination, so predestination, whenever the wicked are treated of, would be understood as a substitute for foreknowledge, if true reason did not object that there cannot be foreknowledge of things that are not. And hence just as God is said to predestine someone to the pains of punishment, in the same way he is stated to have foreknowledge of sins, to such an extent that an almost identical figurative expression is

---

121. Matt. 26.50.
122. John 15.15.
123. Matt. 23.9.
124. *Ibid.* 13.11.

By What Kind of Expressions God Is Said to Have Foreknowledge

used to describe his foreknowledge of sinners and their predestination to torments. However, more usually and more frequently in sacred writings we find him spoken of as having foreknown rather than predestined both sins and punishments. Hence Augustine himself, that most acute investigator and assertor of truth, has taken care to leave us examples of such modes of expression in his models, so that we have no problem about accepting exactly the same meaning in divine predestination and divine foreknowledge, even if we do not exactly find them equally used in those writings.

4. And hence we ought to understand in its truest and most salutary sense what he, as if admonishing us, says:[125] "All predestination is foreknowledge but not all foreknowledge is predestination"; as if he were saying clearly that foreknowledge may not, however, overstep the bounds of predestination, since they are in fact of one and the same, that is divine, nature, in which one thing is not greater or less than another. Rightly so: where there is simplicity of nature there is no diversity, since in it all things are one. Foreknowledge, therefore, has the same importance for God as predestination; plainly so because they are one. Nevertheless, the scripture does not so widely and so frequently make use of the term 'predestination' as of 'foreknowledge'. In fact in the divine works of creation and administration we find foreknowledge and predestination simultaneously and always linked together by an inseparable yoke. In the case of evil things, however, which, since they are not from God, are nothing at all, we find most often the term 'foreknowledge', but rarely 'predestination'. This we must believe to have come about deliberately for our utility. And rightly so, that by this mode of expression we might be reminded that foreknowledge is not one thing, predestination another, but that they are one, seeing that always they are understood simultaneously in those things which by them are created or bestowed; but in the things which are neither substantially carried out by them nor bestowed from the treasure of their generosity, they are understood to be truly absent. Yet foreknowledge is improperly said to be present everywhere, predestination in places only, to the extent that like species in a genus, one is seen in the other, predestination in foreknowledge.

5. But if that should trouble anyone which truth does not cease to impress upon sound minds, namely that God is prescient and the predes-

---

125. Augustine, *De praedestinatione sanctorum* 10, 19.

tinator of all the things that are from him, but not of those which are not from him and are therefore nothing, that person should 'return into himself', look towards what is above, and consult Truth itself. For in that Truth there shines out the essential light, flowing without darkness, of prescient predestination and predestining foreknowledge. No doubt of it, since of God nothing is predicated accidentally. How, then, is the highest essence to be believed to be in those things which are nothing? Come now! If God's foreknowledge is God, necessarily it is Truth too. This I might say of predestination: if it also is God, beyond doubt it is Truth too. But truth, as Augustine says,[126] must be in something, that is in true and lasting things. Accordingly, if foreknowledge and predestination are Truth, but Truth is the truth of true things which on that account are true because by it they are made, foreknowledge and predestination, therefore, pertain only to those things which were made by Truth. If, as I hold, Truth does not pertain to sins, how can foreknowledge or predestination be of them? Further, if Truth is necessarily in true things, in them, therefore, are foreknowledge and predestination. If everything that naturally is is necessarily from the Truth, who would doubt, then, that whatever is not according to nature is not from the Truth? Sin is against nature and therefore not from the Truth, and hence neither from the foreknowledge nor the predestination of it. Concerning sins, then, let us briefly draw a conclusion. If Truth is of true things, but clearly true things are only the things that are, divine foreknowledge and predestination are beyond doubt the Truth of true things. Who would doubt, therefore, that sins are false, unless one doubts that they are not from the Truth. It follows that there can be neither foreknowledge nor predestination of them.

6. That is what there is to say about sin. Let us see about punishment or suffering or destruction or however one can describe the world of unhappiness which justly follows upon sin. We said before, in fact, using the authority of father Augustine, that by the mercy of divine predestination nobody is prepared for torments, although, as has often been repeated already, it is said to predestine the wicked to them. Here, as we have pointed out, predestination is put for foreknowledge either by way of similitude, or by that figure of speech which is called ΥΠΑΛΛΑΓΗ (*hypallage*), which we can call *subalternation*; and fittingly so, because the words are not produced in the same order as the sense. Of this the poet[127]

---

126. Cf. Augustine, *De uera religione* 36, 66; *Soliloquia* I, 15, 29.
127. Cf. Virgil, *Aeneid* III, 61.

By What Kind of Expressions God Is Said to Have Foreknowledge

furnishes an example: "To give the south-winds to the fleet," which is understood the other way around as to give the fleet to the south winds. By means of this figure of speech it would not be inappropriate, therefore, for writers to say that the wicked are predestined to punishment; it would be as if they had said that punishment was predestined for the wicked. It would be so, I say, if reason allowed that punishment be in the literal sense declared to be predestined for the wicked. But if by the same kind of expression as the following will demonstrate, the wicked are said to be predestined to sufferings, as also sufferings are predestined for the wicked, there remains that one mode often mentioned already, which is called *entimema* because that mental concept is always taken by contrariety.

7. Hence, as I have said before, by grammarians it is clearly called ΚΑΤ ΑΝΤΙΦΡΑCΙΝ (by antiphrasis). Examples of it in secular literature are the Fates (*Parcae*—the sparing ones) because they spare none; also a grove (*lucus*) because it gives no light; and other such examples which grammarians propose in single words, but which are found in expressions of the rhetoricians, such as Marcus Tullius in his defence of Ligarius:[128] "A new charge, Gaius Caesar!" Also on the divine summits, again and again this species smiles brighter than light; for example, the apostle: "Forgive me for this unfairness";[129] and, as we cited above: "I shall cast away the wisdom of the wise, and the prudence of the prudent I shall reject."[130] And the lord, in the gospel, said to the Jews concerning John the Baptist: "What are you stepping out into the desert to see, a reed shaken by the winds?"[131] Also to his betrayer: "Friend, for what purpose have you come?"[132] and the other things which, as we have said before, were said as if to a sharer in apostolic grace. These suffice by way of example. Let us return to our theme.

8. The following question is to be considered: whether all that we have said about sin we ought likewise to say about its punishment. We did say that all sins are not from God; rightly so, because they are not according to nature, but against nature. Let us listen to the apostle: "Sin is the sting of death."[133] If, therefore, from the wound of sin, death is necessarily the outcome, plainly from sin there will be death, which is the punish-

---

128. Cicero, *Pro Ligario* I, 1.
129. 2 Cor. 12.13.
130. 1 Cor. 1.19.
131. Matt. 11.7.
132. *Ibid.* 26.50.
133. 1 Cor. 15.56.

ment of sin. And so from where there is sin, from there comes death. Unhappiness follows death. Hence from where there is death, from there comes unhappiness, which is punishment or suffering. Accordingly, there is, so to speak, a kind of unbroken chain of evils linking them all together. For out of the perverse and culpable movement of free choice, one, that is, which abandons the highest good, that is its God, whom it could have delighted in, there came the sin of disobedient pride. Forthwith death followed close on sin, and the unhappiness of punishment followed on death. From all of these who can set us free? The grace of God through Jesus Christ.[134] Those things assuredly are not from him who frees us from them. For if they were from him, they would not be evil but good, as no one doubts. But evil they are. Therefore they cannot be from him. Or is there anyone to whom it is not obvious that things mutually opposed cannot originate from the one source? Certainly indeed from the source of good there will not come evil; from the source of humility there will not come pride; from the spring of justice injustice will never flow: from the principle of life death will never proceed; happiness is not the cause of unhappiness. Finally, the highest essence in no way brings about things that are not: sin, death, punishment are a deficiency of justice, life, happiness; therefore they are not from him who is; and hence, if they are not from him, who would dare to say that there is anything in them?

9. The argument is complete, if I am not mistaken, that both sins and punishments are neither made by God nor foreknown nor predestined by him. For who can understand sins? But just as we say that we know in advance that there will be darkness after sunset, and silence after shouting, and pain after the withdrawal of health, and sadness after joy has passed, and toil as rest is lost, folly when wisdom is lost, and other things of the same kind, which all, as Augustine says,[135] are known by not knowing, ignorance of which is the knowledge of them, so indisputably, holy authority declares that God either foreknew or predestined sins or punishments, which can neither be foreknown nor predestined. For they are recognised as being known not in definitions of their forms, but as being not known in the lack of those forms. Why! Does 'nothing' signify anything other than the thinker's conception of the absence of being. What do darkness and silence signify except the thinker's conception of the

---

134. Rom. 7.24–25.
135. Cf. *De ciuitate Dei* XII, 7.

By What Kind of Expressions God Is Said to Have Foreknowledge

absence of either light or sound? When I say that as the sun glows red over the earth I know there is darkness beneath the earth, I wish to signify nothing more than that light is present above the earth but absent beneath the earth. Whatever I say about them, in my mind the concept represented is of the sun. For whether the sun be present or absent, its mental image will always be present in the memory, which indeed, when the sun is present, receives the name of light, when absent, of darkness. This I say: the conception of it present is called light; the conception of it absent, darkness.

10. These, therefore, and all such images demonstrate only the concept of the absence or deficiency of things that are. Accordingly, the person who is in pain, what does he know except that health is absent? In suffering, therefore, it is not pain itself but health itself that he knows, which certainly he would not know if he had not some conception of it. For the remembrance of health is an abiding perception, but health itself resides in that substance which God created. For the creator does not punish the things he made, nor does he take from them the gifts of nature. For if health was not in some way innate to the nature itself of the sufferer, he would be utterly unaware of it, and the sufferer's memory would not from its unconscious knowledge of it be affected by its absence, nor tormented with longing for its presence. Indeed there is no rational nature which does not wish to escape unhappiness and attain to happiness, nor any which, having once tasted happiness, wants to withdraw from it and live in misery.

CHAPTER SIXTEEN

No Nature Punishes Nature and the Punishments of Sinners Are Nothing Other Than Their Sins

1. Therefore, in the great heat of the eternal fire there should be no other punitive unhappiness than the absence of blessed happiness. Yet there will be no one in that state that has not by nature an innate notion of the happiness that is absent and a yearning for it, so that he is most greatly tormented by that which he ardently strives after, which the just judgment of God does not allow him to grasp. This longing, beyond doubt, would not be in the unhappy one if he was utterly without what he sought after. Therefore, in a most hidden and most true way the damned, in the deepest unhappiness of punishments, will possess happiness and will not possess it. They will, indeed, have some notion of the memory of it, but they will not have its features as the fruit of contemplation. Certainly the unhappy would not have this notion of happiness in their memory, as we have said, if there were not some knowledge of it in their nature. But just as no one has the notion of truth outside of himself, so also the knowledge of it. Truth is happiness. No one, therefore, will possess the notion and knowledge of happiness outside of his own nature. There will, then, be truth in the nature of the unhappy; therefore there will be happiness.

But how will that nature be unhappy in which there will be happiness, which is truth? What? If no nature will have been punished, will it, indeed, be unhappy? I do not imagine so. For what reason will any nature be unhappy if it will not have been punished? Therefore, if no nature can be punished, no nature will be unhappy. But who would not believe that all nature either is God or was made by him? It is the greatest madness to suspect that creative nature is capable of unhappiness. But by what kind of justice creative nature will punish the natures it has itself created I cannot discover. Hence no nature will be punished; if not punished it will not be unhappy.

2. But if anyone is, perhaps, unwilling to yield to this reasoning, he will not, I believe, refute the authority of father Augustine who in Book XI of his Hexaemeron[136] does not hesitate to declare: "It occurs to almost anyone, and it is true and evident that it is contrary to justice itself that God would condemn in anyone, for nothing previously merited, what he himself had created in them; and the sure and obvious damnation of the devil and his angels may be reaffirmed from the gospel, where the lord declared that he would say to those on his left: 'Go into the eternal fire which has been prepared for the devil and his angels.'[137] There it is by no means the nature which God created but the evil personal will which one should believe is to be punished by the pain of eternal fire. Furthermore it is not his nature that is designated where it is said : 'This is the beginning of the creation of the lord which he made so that he is made a mockery of by his angels.'[138] It is either the aerial body which he suitably adapted to such a will. Or it is the arrangement itself in which he made him, even if unwilling, amenable to good things, or by which, with the foreknowledge that he of his own will would be wicked, he nevertheless made him, not holding back his own goodness in providing life and substance, even for the prospective guilty will. For at the same time he foresaw what great good things he would do as a result of it by his own marvellous goodness and power." If, therefore, the angelic nature in the devil may not justly be punished, why wonder if that same divine justice prevents the human substance being punished even in the most wicked men? For one is not justly punished unless one is convicted of an offence. There is no wicked-

---

136. Augustine, *De Genesi ad litteram* XI, 21, 28–XI, 22, 29.
137. Matt. 25.41.
138. Job 40.14.

ness found in any man except the culpable perversity of his own will. That in the truest sense is not nature, because out of God the creator of all things it was created in no substance. It may, then, be justly punished in unhappiness. Hence Augustine:[139] "He is exceedingly wicked and ill-informed who cannot distinguish the imperfection of nature from the author of nature to whom is absolutely alien anything at all that is to be condemned in anyone at all. For he creates men in order that they should be men, and in the multiplication of successions of generations he does not withdraw his workmanship, according to the design of his good will continuing to restore in the many what he himself made, continuing to punish in the many what he himself did not make."

3. Since, therefore, God created in the first man the universal nature of all men, for as yet, as Augustine says,[140] that one man was everyone, that which in him was naturally created could by no means transgress the natural law of the creator. That in him, therefore, did not sin which God created in him; yet in him all men sinned, and hence in him all die and consequently all are punished. Accordingly, it is quite correctly believed that as God wished to create in him the universal substance of the human race, so also he created the individual will of all men. For if in one man there was created, as the totality, both the corporal and spiritual human nature common to all men, there was necessarily in him the individual will of each one. In him, therefore, it was not the generality of nature that sinned but the individual will of each one, because if that nature offended, since it is one, the whole would certainly perish. But it did not perish, since the remedy for the wound, that is the substance of a redeemer, remained in it incorrupt, apart from the fact that all sinned simultaneously in one man. For it was not he that sinned in all, but all in him. For just as he had his own personal will, so also he had his personal sin; and as in him each one had become master of the indivisible individuality of his own will, so in him each one of his own accord was able to commit his personal offence. For in no one is the sin of another justly punished. Accordingly, in no one is nature punished, because it is from God and does not sin. But the motion of the will wantonly misusing that good

---

139. In fact, Prosper of Aquitaine, *Responsiones ad capitula obiectionum Vincentianarum,* obiect. 3 (*PL* XLV, 1845).
140. Augustine, *De ciuitate Dei* XIII, 14; *Enarrationes in Psalmos* 84, 7 (*Expositions on the Book of the Psalms* ACW 29, 30; NPN 8).

of nature is deservedly punished, because it transgresses the law of nature, which beyond doubt it would not transgress if it were substantially created by God.

4. Hence the clear conclusion is that in the wicked it is not what God has made that undergoes punishments, but what pride has corruptly devised. Indeed the passion of a perverse will is tortured when it is not allowed to have those things which it evilly or unworthily strives after; for by this name, that is of concupiscence, the generality of all the vices is understood. But if reason has established that no nature is punished, necessarily it will establish that no nature punishes. For neither as creating nor created does she punish what is created, because no substance can be contrary to the substance of another. Otherwise some nature would be punished most unjustly whose ill merit did not precede its punishment. This clearly Augustine, in the passage quoted above, wanted to make plain, saying that it is contrary to justice itself that, without any preceding ill merit, God should condemn in anyone that very thing which he himself created in him. This reasoning is especially justified from the fact that the authorship of no sin is referred to God except quite erroneously and impiously. But if sin is from nature, but nature from God, surely it would follow that sin is from God. God forbid that we should believe that, or accept that totally invalid argument which thus falsely concludes: All nature is from God; but all sin is from nature: therefore from God is all sin. But if it is quite absurd to concede this, there remains that most true and worthy syllogism, full of charity and catholic faith, which is set out in this way: Every good thing either is God or is made from God; all that is made from God effects no corruption of the good; and conversely: therefore no corruption of the good is from the good. All sin, because it is evil, is a defect of the good; no corruption of the good is from the good; therefore no sin, because it is evil, can be from the good. Every creature sharing in reason is a great good; from no good is evil; therefore sin is from no creature sharing in reason.

5. Hence Truth itself says:[141] "The good man from the good treasure of his heart brings forth good things; the evil man from the evil treasure of his heart brings forth evil," as if it said: every good thing which out of his good thought the good man brings forth is given out of a good treasure, that is from him in whom all the treasures of wisdom and knowledge are

---

141. Matt. 12.35.

hidden. Every evil thing, which out of his evil thought the evil man brings forth, is out of his evil treasure, namely from the pride which is the beginning of every sin.

Speaking about this treasure of wickedness, Augustine in the treatise *On True Religion*[142] says: "But the primal defect of the rational soul is the will to do those things which the highest and innermost truth forbids. Thus man was driven from paradise into this world, that is from eternal things to temporal, from abundance to indigence, from strength to weakness. It was not, therefore, from a substantial good to a substantial evil, because no substance is evil, but from an eternal good to a temporal good, from a spiritual good to a carnal good, from an intelligible good to a sensible good, from the highest good to the lowest good. There is, then, a certain good which, if the rational soul should favour it, it sins, because it is ranked below it. Therefore the sin itself is evil, not that substance which by sinning is favoured. That tree, therefore, which is described as planted in the middle of paradise is not evil. But the transgression of the divine command which, since it has just damnation as a consequence, does have a bearing on the case of the tree which, contrary to the prohibition, was touched and gave the power of distinguishing between good and evil. Because when the soul has been caught up in its own sin, by paying the penalties, it learns what the difference is between the commandment it was unwilling to keep and the sin it committed; and by this means, the evil which it did not learn of by avoidance it learned of by experience, and the good which previously it esteemed less in not submitting to it, it now esteems more eagerly by making a comparison. The corruption of the soul, therefore, is its own act, and the difficulty arising from the corruption is the punishment it suffers. And that is the totality of evil. But to do and to suffer is not a substance. Therefore substance is not evil. Thus water is not evil, nor is the creature which lives in the air; for they are substances; but to jump voluntarily into the water is evil, as is the suffocation which one suffers in drowning. The iron stylus, with one part of which we write and with the other delete, is made by a craftsman, and in its own way is beautiful and suited to our need; but if anyone should wish to write with that part which is for deleting, and delete with the part which is for writing, he would not in any way have made the stylus evil, since rightly it is the action itself which would be blamed. If one should

---

142. Augustine, *De uera religione* 20, 38–39.

set this right, where will be the evil? If anyone should suddenly look at the midday sun, his eyes will be repelled and dazzled. But for that reason will either the sun or the eyes be evil? By no means, for they are substances. But evil is the disordered glance, and likewise the consequent disturbance; there will not be evil when the eyes are restored and gaze in proper order at the light."

And a little earlier in the same treatise:[143] "If it is asked who established the body, let him be asked who is the most beautiful of all; for every species is from him. Who is this, then, but the one God, the one truth, the one salvation of all, and the first and highest essence out of which is everything that is, to the extent that it is, because to the extent that it is, whatever is is good? And thus death is not from God; for God did not make death and does not rejoice in the destruction of the living, because the highest essence brings into being all that is, whence it is called being. But death brings into non-being everything that dies (to the extent in which it dies). For if the things that die died utterly they would without doubt come to nothingness. But they die only to the extent that they share less in being. This could be said more briefly in this way: the more they die, the less they have being. But the body is less than any life at all, since whatever little remains in the species remains by means of life, whether by the life by which is governed any single living thing or that by which is governed the universal nature of the world. The body, therefore, is more subject to death and thus is closer to nothingness. Therefore that life which, delighted by bodily enjoyment, neglects God sinks towards nothingness and that is worthlessness. In this way life becomes carnal and earthly, and for this reason also it is called flesh and earth, and for as long as it is such, it will not possess the kingdom of God, and the objects of its loves will be snatched away from it. For it both loves that which is less than life, for it is body and, because of that sin by which it is loved the thing loved becomes corruptible, so that it flows away and abandons its lover, because the lover also in loving the thing loved has abandoned God. For he disregards God's words of command: "Eat this and do not eat that." It is, therefore, dragged down to punishments, because by loving lower things, it finds its ordered place in the lower regions with the dead, in grief and pain and in the poverty of its own pleasures. For what is the pain that is called bodily but the sudden destruction of the health of that thing

---

143. Augustine, *De uera religione* 11, 21-12, 23.

No Nature Punishes Nature

which by ill use the soul has damaged? But what is the pain that is called spiritual if not the deprivation of the mutable things which the soul has enjoyed or hoped it could enjoy? This is the whole of what is called evil, that is, sin and the punishment of sin." Therefore divine justice does not punish what its own goodness wished to create.

6. Beyond doubt, then, it must be held that no nature is punished by another nature, and in this way that no punishment is carried out by God, and hence that it is not foreknown or predestined by him, although he is often said to have carried it out and to have foreknown or predestined it. For God indeed saw to the training of our understanding both in his scriptures and in commentators on it, so that, as we listened to such modes of discourse, our attention would awake to the understanding of the mystery which is hidden in them, not simply what is shown in the superficial expression of the words. This being so, it deserves to be asked what is punished in the punishing of the unhappy by torments and sufferings, and what it is that metes out the punishment. To this enquiry let the holy father Augustine reply, who speaks as follows in the commentary on Psalm VII:[144] "Let us understand that punishment is meted out to each one from his own sin, and that his wickedness is turned into punishment; and let us not think that that tranquility and ineffable light of God provides from itself the means of punishment for sins, but so orders the sins themselves that the things which were the delights of the sinning man become the instruments of the punishing lord": Augustine thus with beauty and clarity defines it that the instruments for the torture of the wicked are none other than that wickedness itself. Indeed every sin which in this life is begun by man with delight will be completed in the future as penalty, unless he becomes free of it by divine grace, through Jesus Christ lord and saviour of the world, before he passes over from this world. But there is no sin that does not punish the sinner. For in every sinner the original emergence of the sin and the punishment of it are simultaneous; because there is no sin which does not punish itself, secretly in this life, but openly in the other life which is to come.

7. This is most manifestly proved by the argument on virtue. For every virtue must be begun in this life and completed in the future life so that, if it be true virtue, it simultaneously begins to attain its corresponding happiness in secret, but in the open only suffering because of the

---

144. *Id., Enarrationes in Psalmos* 7, 16.

things that oppose it and wish absolutely to do away with it. And that this be so in the course of this life is always inevitable. But in that life in which every pious deed is perfected, when all toiling in the defence of virtue is at an end, virtue itself will be for itself its own peace and happiness.[145] Thus 'by contrariety', therefore, every sin from which divine mercy has not absolved man in the course of this present life outwardly brings voluptuous delight to the miserable sinner who persists in it, but inwardly it is punishing itself. But in the future when the fulness of wickedness is accomplished, all those things which here had been the delights of committing sin will be turned into instruments for punishing sin. Sin, therefore, begins here in secret to be punished expressly by sin, and there its punishment will be openly completed; here the beginning of sorrows, there the completion of punishment; here false joy rising from wilful passion, there true sadness from necessary suffering. For deservedly the destructive sweetness of passion here will be turned there into the bitterness of punishment, because here he had wished in wicked pride to turn to the practices of shame the gift of divine generosity. That gift is the free choice of the will which is the natural gift of understanding, that is, of the eye of the mind which the creator bestowed on all in general in order that they might seek, love and enjoy him. But over there, lest he should at all enjoy the nobility of truth, he most justly loses that gift, and in that prison of his own wickedness in which he had enclosed himself, he will not avoid the inescapable punishment that consists in the darkness of eternal ignorance.

8. That is why Augustine in the treatise *On True Religion*[146] says: "Those, therefore, who misuse such a great good as the mind, so that outside it they seek for visible things, by which they ought rather to have been reminded to behold and love intelligible realities, to such people will be given exterior darkness. For the beginning of this darkness is the wisdom of the flesh and the frailty of the bodily senses, with the consequence that those who take pleasure in conflict will be estranged from peace and entangled in the greatest troubles. For the beginning of the greatest trouble is war and contention, and the binding of their hands and feet means, I believe, that all opportunity for action is taken away, and

---

145. A marginal note at this point in the Paris manuscript observes that the writer is identifying virtue as the happiness of man. This would seem to apply to the remainder of the passage.

146. Augustine, *De uera religione* 54, 104–105.

No Nature Punishes Nature

those who want to be thirsty and hungry and to be aroused to passion and relaxed into its fatigue, so that they may cheerfully eat and drink and lie down together and fall asleep, are really in love with that deprivation which is the beginning of extreme sorrow. Therefore, what they love will be accomplished in them, so that for them there will be weeping and gnashing of teeth. For there are many who delight in all these beginnings at the same time, and whose life is spectacle, competition, eating, drinking, sexual intercourse and sleep. In their thoughts they embrace nothing but the phantasm which they gather together from such a way of life; and from the illusion of those phantasms or wickedness they devise rules of superstition and ungodliness by which they are deceived and to which they adhere, even if they attempt to abstain from the allurements of the flesh. For they do not make good use of the talent entrusted to them, that is, the eye of the mind by which all who are called learned or cultivated or refined are seen to excel. Instead they keep the talent tied up in a handkerchief or buried in the ground, that is, enveloped and smothered in superfluous luxuries or worldly desires. Therefore their hands and feet will be bound, and they will be sent into outer darkness, where there will be weeping and gnashing of teeth, not because these are what they loved—for who could love them?—but because the things they did love are the beginnings of these and necessarily lead those who love them towards these others. For those who prefer journeying to returning or arriving, must be sent into faraway places because they are flesh and spirit on the move and not turning back."[147]

9. The holy and truth-loving Pope Gregory agrees with this in Book XI[148] on Job when he comments as follows on the words 'If he shall have closed man in, there is none who can open':[149] "through the fact that he performs an evil act, what does any man do but make a prison of his own conscience, so that guilt of soul oppresses him even if no one from outside makes an accusation? When he is left in the blindness of his wickedness by God in judgment, it is, as it were, within himself that he is locked, lest he find any place of escape, which he in no way deserves to find. For often some people are anxious to get out from their perverse actions, but because they are overwhelmed by the weight of those same

---

147. Ps. 77.39.
148. Gregory the Great, *Moralia in Job* XI, 9 (*PL* 75, 959 A14–C11).
149. Job 12.14, 18.

actions, shut up in the prison of evil habit, they cannot get out from themselves. And indeed, while wanting to punish their own faults by what they consider proper behaviour, turn to more serious sins, and the pitiable result is that what they regarded as a way out they find is closing them in. So for instance the false Judas, when he brought about his own death to counteract his sin, attained the punishment of eternal death, his means of repentance being worse than the sin he committed. Therefore let it be said 'If he shall have closed man in, there is none who can open,' because just as no one resists his generosity when he calls, so none stands against his justice when he abandons. To close in, therefore, means not to open up for those already closed in. Hence also the words about Pharaoh addressed to Moses: 'I shall harden his heart.'[150] For he is said to harden through justice when he does not soften the false heart through grace. Therefore he closes in the man whom he leaves in the darkness of his own deeds." Also in the same work: "'Therefore he unloosed the sword-belt of the kings,' since in those who seemed to govern well their own members, for the sin of self-exaltation he destroyed the girdle of chastity. And what is understood by the rope except sin, as is said through Solomon: 'His own iniquities make the wicked man captive, and he is tied up with the ropes of his own sins.'"[151]

150. Exod. 4.21.
151. Prov. 5.22.

CHAPTER SEVENTEEN

Why God Is Said to Have Predestined Punishments although He Neither Makes nor Predestines Them

1. Accordingly, it is established by reason and authority that it must be firmly held that God, in a word, is not in any way the author of the punishments by which proud wickedness will be racked by eternal torment, that is to say he is in no way their maker, in no way their predestinator. Yet he is called their author and maker and predestinator, by that mode of reasoning by which he is most truly believed to be the maker and governor of the whole universe in which they are. Indeed before he created it he predestined that the state of his universal creation would be one of such beauty that the ugliness of the wicked, which he did not predestine because he did not intend to create it, did not deface the whole: the malice of offenders did no injury, the uncertainty of those in error did not spread doubt, the unhappiness of those worthy of punishment did not disturb the happiness of the elect. For the baseness of the malice, or the error or the unhappiness of no man is allowed to bring dishonour upon the natural order predestined before all ages.

TREATISE ON DIVINE PREDESTINATION

2. When therefore we hear that God predestined one person or another to destruction or suffering or punishment or torture, or whatever name is used to describe the unhappiness by which wickedness is tormented by itself, in itself, through itself, we are required to understand only that he himself before time began foreknew and predestined in what arrangement of the universe they will be whom, by a most secret yet most just judgment, he permitted to experience the bitterness of their sins, because he left them in the first damnable sin, preserving however that most notable difference between foreknowledge and predestination, with the consequence that, while predestination has as wide a scope as foreknowledge, both indeed signifying one and the same thing, that is, divine substance, predestination pertains only to those things which are good, but foreknowledge to good things and bad. Yet that difference is not from nature but from the use of words.

3. For as it is said of God that he is everywhere by the presence of his power but not everywhere by the grace of his dwelling,[152] so it may be said of him that he is everywhere by foreknowledge but not everywhere by predestination. For clearly truth proclaims of God that wheresoever God will have been by his presence, there surely he will be by his dwelling: likewise wherever he will have been by foreknowledge there surely he will be by predestination. Accordingly, just as the presence and dwelling of God is only in those things which were made by him, so his foreknowledge and predestination are to be believed only of those things which he himself would make. And in this way, just as his presence and dwelling are said 'by contrariety' to be in those things which are neither from him nor made by him, although they are not in them, so his foreknowledge and predestination are 'by contrariety' declared present in those things which he neither made nor bestowed because they are nothing. Yet they are not incongruously considered to be in these things which have arisen by a defect of the creature, since not only does he wisely govern the creature itself but he also does not permit its defect to transgress his laws.

4. But that the deeply hidden sufferings of men and the blackest oppressions of the sons of Adam in this mortal life do not cease secretly to punish even those who desire to lead a good life, blessed Augustine clearly wished to show in the eighth book of his *Confessions*[153] where he laments

---

152. Cf. Augustine, *Epistulae* 187, 5, 16 (*Letters*, vol. 4, FC 30; selections E 6, 13; NPN 1).
153. *Id., Confessiones* VIII, 10, 22.

Why God Is Said to Have Predestined Punishments

the force of human unhappiness in himself: "It was I," he says, "while I was resolving now to serve my lord as I had long since determined, it was I myself who wanted to, I who did not want to; it was I, and I did not fully want to nor fully not want to, and so I was struggling with myself and I was being dissipated from myself; and that dissipation, too, was happening against my will, and yet did not demonstrate the nature of another mind in me but the pain of my own; and thus no longer was it I who controlled it, but the sin that dwells in me from the punishment of a more unrestricted sin, because I was the son of Adam." He does not, then, punish, when for those who wound themselves and endure the bitterness of their own offences in themselves, he most honourably arranges those ordered positions in the world in which it most properly becomes them to suffer.

5. Let us, then, apply a sort of parable. Suppose that the master of a great household wishes to build for himself by his own skill a splendid residence, spacious in length, breadth and the extent of its depth, harmonious in the variety of its sides, angles, vaults and of its different perspectives, firm in the depth of its foundations and well designed in the lines of its bases, columns and capitals. Let it also be outstanding in the exalted height of its arches and many-shaped ceilings, consummate in the soaring peaks of its towers, outside and within adorned with the beauty of countless colours and forms in the great variety of its paintings, packed full and embellished with precious metals and costly gems, lit up by the profusion of light shed through variegated and different kinds of windows, and all else that pertains to the adornment of beauty, too lengthy to mention. And so in it no area is to be found which does not captivate all its inhabitants by its amplitude, no part which does not feed the eyes of all who gaze on it with its beauty, no place which is not set off by the clearest light shed on all sides, reflecting back the brightness of gold and gems from its surface, and drawing marvellous colours from them, no spot in it which is not regal, fit for dignity and rest. Finally, if in so great and so marvellous a dwelling, as we have said, the father himself, that is the originator and governor of it, settled his children in one style, his servants in another, those endowed with the gift of perpetual good health in another, in another those tormented by the helplessness of the evil desires which by the excess of their own passion they had brought upon themselves, hissing through their teeth, swarming with worms, afflicted by all the different kinds of everlasting grief; should he rightly be regarded as the harshest torturer who was praised as the most just governor? And indeed

it was his duty not to mix together those of different rank in his household lest he might seem to those of perverse view to punish those whom he governs. But what form of punishments would he be convicted of carrying out who wished all that he made to be made, not for the purposes of unhappiness, but for the completeness of the world and for the grace of its beauty?

6. Hence Augustine in his treatise *On True Religion*[154] says: "An imperfection of the soul is not its nature but against its nature, and is nothing other than sin and the punishment of sin. From this it is understood that no nature, or to express it better, no substance or essence, is evil, nor does it come about from the sins and punishments of the soul that the universe is defiled by any deformity, because the rational substance which is unstained by any sin, being subject to God, governs those other things which are subject to itself. But that which has committed sin is given its ordered place where it is proper that such should be, so that all things may be seemly, God being the creator and ruler of the universe. And the beauty of the created world is faultless because of these three things, the condemnation of sinners, the testing of the just, the perfecting of the blessed." And a little later, speaking of the soul, he says: "But by its own failing it collapses into more corruptible beauties, that is, into the corresponding level of punishments. And let us not wonder that up to now I speak of beauties. For nothing is in order which is not beautiful. And as the apostle says: 'All order is from God.'"[155]

7. "What wonder is it, then, if the soul of man which, wherever it may be, and whatever kind it may be, is better than any body. I shall say that it is beautifully ordered and that other beauties are made from its punishments, since when it is unhappy it is not where it is proper for the happy to be, but where it is fitting for the unhappy to be." Accordingly, by no part of the universe is the wicked man punished but by his own wickedness in himself, as the opinions of the holy fathers cited earlier bear witness. For God did not make the sun with a view to its damaging by its rays the sight of one who looks at it in an uncontrolled way and beating them back into darkness, which is certainly due not to it but to the disordered gaze itself; nor does he torture the one suffering severe pain in the eyes, since in his suffering nothing hurts him as much as the brilliance of

---

154. Id., *De uera religione* 23, 44; 41, 77.
155. Rom. 13.1.

the sun, while the suffering itself does not by the nature of things outwardly touch the sufferer, but inwardly racks him by some corruption of the bodily health. So in the same way that eternal fire which is prepared for the devil and his angels was certainly in no way created for this purpose, especially if it is the fourth element of the world; it is believed with greater probability to have been created for the completeness of the world, which God foresaw was to be made, rather than for burning up the wicked man for whom his own pride would serve as sufficient punishment. This further argument[156] can be added that, although he was first created by God in an ethereal body in which nothing could suffer, this ethereal body, when it was swollen with pride, was thrust out from the celestial abodes, that is, the upper world, into this air dense with moisture, of vaporous gloom, subject to disturbances, so that from then on a body in keeping with his deserts was joined to him against his will, and for this reason he is punished in it by his own wickedness.

8. Either corporeal fire, then, as Augustine says,[157] or incorporeal, as is Gregory's view,[158] (in keeping, as I think, with his own subtlety) is said to be predestined or prepared for the devil, for the reason that in it he was to be allotted his due place of punishment with all his partners in evil. And just as that same fire, good surely because made by one who is good, should be called evil for no other reason than because in it the bad are settled in most due order, in that way also it is not unsuitably declared a punishment, because those same bad ones in that same place are painfully and pitiably tormented by their own wantonly committed crimes. That fire is not, therefore, a punishment nor prepared or predestined for that purpose; but what had been predestined to be in the universe of all good things became the abode of the wicked. In it beyond doubt there will dwell the blessed no less than the damned; but just as one and the same light, as we have said, is suited to healthy eyes, but hampers those in pain, one and the same food or drink is bitter in the throat of the feeble, pleasant in the throat of those who enjoy good health, so indeed the unimpaired joy of their salvation pleases the former, the punitive sadness of their corruption displeases the latter. One and the same water sustains the swimmer and suffocates the drowning man. Of two people placed in

---

156. Cf. Augustine, *De Genesi ad litteram* III, 10, 14; XI, 26, 33; *De trinitate* III, 7, 12; *De natura boni* 33, 33; *De ciuitate Dei* VIII, 14–15, XXI, 10, 1.
157. *De ciuitate Dei* XXI, 10, 2.
158. Gregory the Great, *op. cit.*, XV, 29.

one and the same spot in a royal court one catches a fever, the other experiences pleasure; to the one who is rejoicing, all the adornments in the whole palace give delight and pleasure, have a praiseworthy appearance, are in estimable harmony; to the fevered man, on fire within himself from his illness, of all that he sees outside himself nothing delights him, nothing is praiseworthy: for he censures everything, and nothing is agreeable because he is in dread of everything. Rightly so: for what good thing would not injure him, when the maker of all good could not please him? Or when will no good thing not injure one whom it has not pleased to enjoy the highest good?

9. Accordingly, if there is no happiness except eternal life, and eternal life is the knowledge of truth, therefore there is no happiness except the knowledge of truth. But in case that syllogism in any way raises doubts in our minds, let us listen to Truth itself clearly proclaiming it: "He who loves me will be loved by my father and I will love and will show myself to him."[159] Also in another place: "But this is eternal life, that they may know you the one true God and Jesus Christ whom you have sent."[160] But whatever is believed concerning happiness must be believed 'by contrariety' about its absence, that is, unhappiness. Thus if there is no unhappiness except eternal death: and eternal death is ignorance of the truth: then there is no unhappiness except ignorance of the truth. Therefore, where truth is not known, there there is no life. But where there is no life, there uninterrupted death must be at hand. If these things should be so, who would dare to say that God is the predestinator of punishment, except one who is rash enough to declare him the author of ignorance, despite the fact that from him is all understanding. Therefore each one is punished by his own obstinacy, which is in no way from God; and for this reason in no way should he be believed to be its author.

159. John 14.21.
160. *Ibid.* 17.3.

CHAPTER EIGHTEEN

The Error of Those Whose Thinking on Predestination Disagrees with That of the Holy Fathers Has Grown out of an Ignorance of the Liberal Arts

1. I would think, therefore, that the gravest error of those who confusedly, and hence fatally, reduce to their own distorted meaning the opinions of the venerable fathers, and for the most part Saint Augustine, had its beginnings from an ignorance of the useful arts which wisdom itself wanted to be its own companions and investigators, and on top of that, ignorance also of Greek writings in which the interpretation of predestination generates no mist of ambiguity. If these things are more carefully considered by those who enquire into truth, not by those who maintain falsehood, then as often as predestination, whether of the good in ordinary language, or of the bad in figurative language, unveils the first sight of its countenance, very familiar to the wise, indeed, but concealed from those swollen by the infection of pride, it will certainly reveal it fully, with no intervening hindrance to those of pious understanding.

TREATISE ON DIVINE PREDESTINATION

2. There is, then, a word among the Greeks ωPω which among the Latins is expressed by three words : for ωPω is interpreted as 'I see' (*uideo*) and 'I define' (*diffinio*) and 'I destine' (*destino*): similarly its composite ΠPOωPω 'I foresee' (*praeuideo*), 'I predefine' (*praediffinio*), 'I predestine' (*praedestino*). This is very easily deduced from the constructions of holy scripture: in the epistle to the Romans:[161] TOY OPICΘENTOC YIOY ΘEOY EN ΔINAMEI, 'of the son of God destined in power'; and in the epistle to the Ephesians:[162] EN AΓAΠE ΠPOωPICAC HMAC, 'in charity predestining us'; and a little further on: ΠPOωPICTHNTEC KATA ΠPOCΘHCIN ΘEOY, 'predestined according to God's plan'. In all these the translator has used the word *predestination*, although he could also have used the others, that is *foresight* and *predefinition*, since these three words, as we have said, express the meaning of one Greek word. Hence that noun ωPOCIA or ΠPOωPOCIA which for them is derived from the verb ωPω or ΠPOωPω among us is called 'vision' (*uisio*) or 'definition' (*diffinitio*) or 'determining' (*destinatio*), and their composites 'foresight', 'predefinition', 'predestination', come from the Greek compound, which is ΠPOωPOCIA. From this it is clearly shown that in these three words there is either the same sense or so great a closeness in meaning that any one of them can be put in the place of the other.

3. This reasoning is confirmed in the strongest way by the expressions of Saint Augustine. For when, in the book called ENKEIPIΔON (The Handbook on Faith, Hope and Charity)[163] he was expounding the verse of the psalmist, "Great the works of the lord sought out by all his wills,"[164] he writes, among other things: "Whom he justly predestined to punishment"; and immediately after: "whom he favourably predestined to grace." Expounding the same verse in the same way in the EXHMEPωN (Hexaemeron),[165] Book XI, he says: "Great the work of the lord, sought out by all his wills. He foresees those who will be good and creates them; he foresees those who will be bad and creates them, offering himself to the

---

161. Rom. 1.4.
162. Eph. 1.5; 1.11. These Latin versions are attested in *Vetus Latina* 24/1, 13 and 24–25; *Vetus Latina* for Rom. (note 1 above) is not to hand. Madec (ed., p.111, note) takes the Greek forms throughout this passage to be the work of Eriugena himself and not imputable to a scribe.
163. Augustine, *Enchiridion* 26, 100.
164. Ps. 110.2.
165. Augustine, *De Genesi ad litteram* XI, 11, 15.

good to enjoy, lavishing on the bad also many of his gifts, mercifully pardoning them, justly punishing them; also mercifully punishing them, justly pardoning them; not apprehensive of anyone's malice, not standing in need of anyone's justice, seeking no benefit to himself even from the works of the good, and seeking benefit for the good even from the punishments of the bad." Here assuredly it should be understood that he meant nothing else by the word 'predestination' than what he meant by the word 'foresight'.

4. Who, then, but a madman would not see that for God to predestine is nothing else than to predefine, and to predefine is not other than to foresee; therefore to predestine is not other than to foresee. Accordingly, just as we say that God foresaw what he would make and what he would not make, since beyond doubt the things he would not make are nothing—for all things were made by him, and without him was made nothing; but nothing cannot be seen—so we often find writers saying that God predestined what he would make and what he would not make and predefined likewise. For if in Greek manuscripts, coming upon ΠΡΟѠPICEN we do not hesitate to understand 'he foresaw' or 'he predefined' or 'he predestined', what prevents us, when we hear 'he predestined', from interpreting it as 'he foresaw' or 'he predefined', without prejudice to that immutable reasoning by which these and suchlike words are understood to apply only in these things which God made, but can be said 'by contrariety' to be in those which God did not make since they are not?

O eternal truth[166] and true charity, show yourself to those who seek you in all the things in which you are! Show, o creative wisdom, that there is nothing outside you, and that all things that are within you are only those foreseen and predestined, predefined and foreknown, but those things which are said to be, although they are not, are not from you, nor are they in you, and therefore not predestined nor predefined nor foreknown nor foreseen by you. O most merciful lord, you did not make sin, nor death, nor destruction, nor punishment, and so they are not, and there cannot come from you what you did not wish to be made. You do not wish for the death of the sinner, but you do wish that he be converted and live. O eternal wisdom, grant that anyone who sees that he who is creative life in no way made the death of created life, since if it were to

---

166. For this passage cf. Augustine, e.g., *Confessiones* VII, 10, 16.

die it would not suffer punishments. But if the sinful soul does suffer punishments, that proves that it lives.

5. Therefore the death of the soul is sin; God did not make sin for the soul, since he it is who frees it from sin; and so life did not make the death of life. The penalty for sin is death; God did not make death; therefore he did not make the penalty. Torment is a penalty; God did not make a penalty; therefore he did not make torment. The penalty for sin is death; the death of life is sin; therefore the penalty for sin is sin. Penalty is suffering; therefore the suffering of sin is sin. Eternal life is Jesus Christ; Jesus Christ is the death of eternal death; therefore eternal life is the death of eternal death, just as he himself said: "I will be your death, O death, and your bite, O hell."[167] Accordingly life is not the death of life, which he made, but it is the death of the death which he destroyed in those whom he predestined to enjoy him. But in those whom he predestined to perish he did not destroy death, because he left them in the 'mass' of original sin, by his own judgment so very remote from our understanding; having left them he abandoned them; abandoned by the light, darkness torments them; abandoned by life death destroys them. What he made in them he did not leave or abandon, otherwise their nature would return to nothing, if the highest being were not in them; but what he did not make in them, that is to say, pride, he spurned. For God always dwells in that nature which he created for himself, and in this way that nature always remains in which he, who always is, abides.

6. But when I used the expression—"those whom he predestined to destruction"—I used it because, finding that blessed Augustine often used such an expression, I intended to show, with God's help, what was meant to be conveyed in such a mode of expression by that pious father of doctrine, that most illustrious model of eloquence, that keenest enquirer into truth, that most zealous teacher of the liberal arts, that wisest stimulator of minds and humblest persuader, lest any might think that in what he said he intended what is seen to be opposed to the truth. He did not, then, wish his words, "those whom he justly predestined to punishment," to be understood in the same way as his words, "those whom he favourably predestined to grace." Take note of these words that follow. All creation, before it was made, was so predestined, that is, predefined and foreseen, by the creator that it entirely fulfilled the limits of its own nature, within

---

167. Hosea 13.14.

which it was to have been created, and in no way exceeded them. But the limits of all natures are determined in the art of the almighty artist which is the wisdom of the father, in which and through which all things were created. Next there are some created natures which neither wish nor are able to transgress the order of eternal law, such as are all the things which lack reason and intellect. But there are also some in which reason and intellect are substantially implanted. Of these one part, indeed, freed by the grace of its creator, voluntarily obeys the eternal laws and by cleaving to them is made happy; but the other, deservedly abandoned to pride and disobedience, refused to be confined within the order of the forementioned divine law, but it was unable to surmount it. For in whatever way the rational will basely moves, it will find in the eternal art[168] the limit within which its baseness will be honourably ordered, in such a way that from its own hateful wickedness the laudable discipline of wisdom is honoured, and the disordered deformity of one part does not diminish the supremely ordered beauty of the whole.

7. Accordingly, the supreme and ineffable divine wisdom predestined limits in its laws beyond which the wickedness of the ungodly cannot advance. For no one's wickedness is allowed to extend to infinity, as he might wish, since the divine laws impose a limit to his advance. For to what does that worthlessness of all impious men and of their chief, the devil, aspire if not to withdraw from that which is the highest essence, to the extent that their nature, if divine law allowed, would return to nothingness? For this is why it is called worthlessness (*nequitia*)[169] because it strives to be to no purpose (*nequiquam*), that is, nothingness. But since difficulty arising from the eternal laws prevents it from falling as greatly as it would wish, by that difficulty it is oppressed, and in its oppression it is tormented, punished, tortured. And whence does it become unhappy? From the indigence of empty pleasure. Therefore God predestined the ungodly to punishment or destruction, that is, he circumscribed them by his immutable laws which their impiety is not allowed to elude. That is, he ordered them to their own punishment: for, as has been said, that very difficulty by which they are prevented from attaining to what they wantonly strive after, becomes for them penal ruin and the just torment of their wretched passions. Indeed, just as God freed the will of the elect whom he

---

168. For this expression cf. Augustine, *De vera religione* 31, 57.
169. Again Eriugena is indebted to Augustine, *op. cit.*, 11, 21.

predestined to grace, and filled it with the compassion of his love, so that not only are they glad to be confined within the bounds of the eternal law, but do not even doubt that the greatest gift of his glory is that they are neither willing nor able to overstep them; in the same way he represses the will of those rejected, whom he predestined to the most shameful punishment, so that, contrariwise, whatever pertains to the joy of the happy life is for them turned into the torment of unhappiness.

8. Therefore of each part a number is predestined: indeed God created in each a substantial portion of nature and predefined what was created. For one and the same nature is numerically multiplied in all, so that the one is in each, and each is in the one, and the one itself is not other than each, and each is not other than the one. Of all these, then, that God created, a number is predestined: but since the creator foresaw that that number itself would generically perish in the first man, save for the remedy for the wound which is Christ, he predestined, that is before they were made he defined, both the number of them which by his grace he would set free and the number of them which by his justice he would abandon. For he intended to bestow on the former the gifts of his mercy, to fulfil in the latter that portion of nature by which the universe would be perfected and to manifest in both cases the wealth of his goodness, granting to all the power of keeping his laws, if they so willed, before all sinned in one man, but not granting to all to so will. After the sin he would prepare the elect for happiness, disposing the rejected so as to keep his laws, albeit unwillingly, although he did not predestine them to be made to serve him in that way, but to cleave to him with a perfect willingness; but they serve him against their will, not by their nature, which he made in them and does not punish in them, but by the bad will which he did not make and does punish in them. For in that they serve him against their will, they are punished in themselves by their own suffering, for which God in some way prepares those whom he justly does not set free, in permitting them to prepare themselves for it. For truth teaches both that he has predestined no one to destruction and prepared destruction for no one.

9. And so he predestined that the ungodly would against their will respect his eternal and most just laws and not transgress them by any impulse of their own impiety with its tendency towards the depths of evil, and by that mode of punishing they would perish. For no heavier penalty is inflicted on a wicked servant than that he be forced against his will to serve a just master. For inwardly in himself he suffers more from the in-

citement of a proud will than exteriorly from the harshest lashing of his body, because when he is not allowed to spurn the will of his master, he is tormented by himself within himself. But what person of proper judgment would ascribe the origin of such a punishment to the just master and not rather to the unjust servant? For indeed he is set on fire within himself by the torches of his own disobedience before the master from outside adds any torment to the sum of the punishment. God is said, then, to have predestined the ungodly to ruin, in that mode of speech by which he could be said to circumscribe by his laws the impiety by which they perish and by the just restraint of his direction to have checked the impulse of their wanton pride, so that in a marvellous and ineffable manner the beauteous direction exercised by the divine laws would be the worst condemnation of their wickedness. Just as one and the same law establishing the state by the most equitable order brings life to those willing to live well, so it brings ruin to those who desire to lead an evil life. Within those same walls of the royal palace the fevered man is tortured by his unhappiness, the man with strong health rejoices. Of the two who at the same time look at the sun, the one with ordered gaze is illuminated, the disordered one is stricken by darkness. One and the same food is bitter for the sick, sweet for the healthy; one and the same spiritual teaching is for some the odour of life leading to life, for others the odour of death leading to death.

10. And so divine predestination, which, assuredly, is nothing other than divine foresight, made all things that it willed. It established all things substantially and ordered all things by its own most beauteous, most just and most merciful laws, in order that those set free through the only begotten son of God, our lord Jesus Christ, would freely and blessedly reign in them. But those abandoned by him would against their will obey them, and for this reason would perish under them; and the result would not be that anything of their nature, which he made, would perish, but that in them what he did not make would be compelled to be punished. Whenever, then, I hear the words: "these whom he justly predestined to punishment," I understand them to mean those whose wickedness, by which they are punished, he predestined to be held in by his laws. For, just as he in no way predestined the wicked to wickedness, so in no way did he predestine wickedness for the punishment of the wicked. And just as he predestined that the wicked would observe his laws against their will, so he predestined that the wicked, punished by their own wickedness, would

not escape his laws. Here it is subtly to be understood that predestination is itself the law, and the law itself is predestination. For if all predestination is definition and all law definition, then all predestination is law and all law predestination. Therefore divine predestination is the eternal law of all natures and the unchangeable system mercifully restoring the ruins of a changeable creation in those whom by his grace he elected, but in powerful control of those whom he justly repelled. Thus, while the system itself is the same, remaining always unvarying in itself, for those who love it it is the glory of happiness, for those who hate it it is the reproach of punishments; and while the happiness of those who love it is nothing other than joy in the truth, the unhappiness of those who hate it is nothing other than pain from the equity of truth. Their own envy torments the latter against their will; their own love crowns the good will of the former.

CHAPTER NINETEEN

Eternal Fire

1. Concerning eternal fire, however, of which the lord says in the gospel: "Go, ye accursed, into the eternal fire which was prepared for the devil and his angels,"[170] no one must doubt that it is corporeal, although by virtue of the subtlety of its nature it is called incorporeal, just as we are in the habit of calling the region of air 'spirit' although it is the fourth of the corporeal creation. Nor would I easily believe that another fire was prepared for punishing the devil with all his 'limbs', apart from the one which is the fourth element of the world. Why! Those bodies of the ungodly which certainly are composed of those four corporeal elements, must be released back into them at a particular predefined time and be recalled once again from them at the moment of resurrection. Is it any wonder, then, if in that fire where the bodies of all which are to rise again will most substantially endure, those bodies should deservedly suffer the eternal punishments of their wickedness?

2. Here it is not inappropriate to believe that the bodies of the saints will be changed into an ethereal quality which cannot be consumed by another quality, although it can change the qualities of inferior bodies into itself; but the bodies of the ungodly will pass over into a lower airy quality

---

170. Matt. 25.41.

and so suffer from fire which is higher. Hence it is that the devil after his fall, being thrust from the ethereal region, had added to him against his will a body of lower air in which to pay the penalties of his pride. And in a wonderful and ineffable mode of the natures it is brought about, by a hidden yet just judgment, that what the elements of the world, intertwined with one another and inseparably joined together, as it were, by a certain bond of natural love, strive for in a supremely ordered movement is changed into punishment for those who hate the truth. For the superior fiery quality, by its natural force seeks always by its natural motion to transfuse into itself the qualities of the inferior elements, as if as a kind of nourishment for itself.

3. Since therefore, as we have said, the highest quality of all bodies, which is that of the upper air, both confines the inferior qualities by encompassing them and, as the law of nature permits, never ceases to absorb them into itself, there is marvellously achieved the joy of the natures within themselves, but unspeakable torture of evil wills. Accordingly, the bodies of all the ungodly, that is of perverse men and angels, will endure the punishments of eternal fire in such a way that the integrity of their substance will in no way perish, their beauty will in no way fail, their natural soundness will remain; finally all the good things of their nature by a wonderful ordering will shine bright for the adornment of the universe, except for that happiness of which they will be deprived, which is not from nature but from grace. As the quality of the higher corporeal fire clashes with the bodies of the lower air, it maintains its natural force, and the consciousness of the unhappy souls suffers eternal tribulations from their own bodies. So it comes about that all bodies are made glorious by that very same fire by which punishment will be heaped up from outside upon souls damned from within by their own wickedness.

4. But if it seems incredible to anyone that bodies will, indeed, burn forever and nothing of their nature will perish, let him consider that stone which is found in Arcadia beneath the mountain of Erimanthus:[171] this stone being of an iron brightness is set on fire by a touch but cannot be burned away. The Greeks, in fact, call it *asbestos*, that is, inextinguishable, with the result that it acquires even a colour of a fiery nature and there is no reduction of its substance. Consider also the salamander, that

---

171. Cf. Augustine, *De ciuitate Dei* XXI, 5,1; Isidore of Seville, *Etymologiae* XIV, 4, 15.

Eternal Fire

lives in fire.[172] Hence it can be inferred that it is neither substance nor its qualities that are to be tormented by the fire of hell, but that it is the bodily senses of the sufferer and his recalcitrant spirit that will wrestle with eternal misery.

---

172. Cf. Augustine, *op. cit.* XXI, 4, 1.

EPILOGUE

Divine Predestination

1. And so, behold I worship one God, the one beginning of all things and the wisdom whereby every soul that is wise is wise, and by whose very favour all happy things are happy.[173] I acknowledge his one and only and true predestination, which is what he himself is. For his law is eternal and immutable, and just as it has predestined no one to wickedness, for it is good, so it has predestined no one to ruin, for it is life. And, conversely, just as it has not predestined wickedness, which is ruin, for any wicked man, so it has predestined ruin, which is wickedness, for no wicked man. For no catholic is permitted to believe that the highest good, which is the source of every good thing, has predestined any wickedness for anyone, or that the highest life, from which, and in which, and through which all things live, has predestined ruin or punishment for anyone, seeing that it does not allow to perish even that which, turning against itself, destroys itself.

2. Accordingly, whenever I hear those who proclaim you, o most blessed truth, the common life of all, saying that you have predestined the ungodly for ruin, or ruin for the ungodly, immediately, o brightest light, as you illuminate my darkness, in you I see that you predestined, that is, before time began, you defined within your immutable laws, a certain

---

173. Augustine, *De vera religione* 55, 112 (*uerbatim*).

number of those who would perish in their own ungodliness, which ungodliness you never and nowhere predestined. Or to express it in another way: you, O lord, have predestined, in your infallible and unalterable foreknowledge, the number of those who were to prepare both the punishment of their own ungodliness and their own ruin, in whom you were to punish not what you made, but to abandon to punishment what you did not make. This, o eternal life of minds, is my belief concerning your predestination, which you yourself are.

3. And for this reason, in company with all right thinking believers, I anathematize those who say that there are two predestinations, or one which is twin, or in two parts, or double. For if there are two, it is not one divine substance; if twin, it is not indivisible; if in two parts, it is not simple but composed of parts; if double, it is multiple. And if we are forbidden to call the divine unity triple, by what kind of madness does the heretic dare to call it double? Therefore, having cast from our hearts this monstrous, poisonous, deadly doctrine, let us believe that the one eternal predestinaion of God is God, and exists only in those things that are, but has no bearing at all on those that are not.

Bibliography

The references to St. Augustine in the notes are based, for the most part, on the footnotes of G. Madec to his 1978 edition of the text. The information on English-language versions of Augustinian texts is derived almost entirely from J. J. O'Meara, *An Augustine Reader* (New York, 1973), pp. 545–53 (Bibliographical Guide).

Manuscript

d'Alverny, M.-Th. "Les Solutiones ad Chosroem de Priscianus Lydus et Jean Scot." In *Jean Scot Érigène et l'histoire de la philosophie: actes du Colloque international du Centre national de la recherche scientifique, Laon, juillet 1975* (hereafter cited as *Jean Scot Érigène et l'histoire de la philosophie*), ed. R. Roques, pp. 145–60. Paris, 1977. (This is a description of Paris, Bibliothèque nationale, MS lat. 13386).

Editions

Floss, H. J., ed. *Joannis Scoti opera quae supersunt omnia*. PL 122. Paris, 1853.
Madec, G., ed. *Iohannis Scotti: De diuina praedestinatione liber*. Corpus Christianorum, Continuatio medievalis, number 50. Turnhout, 1978.

Bibliography

Maugin, G. *Veterum auctorum qui ix. saeculo de praedestinatione et gratia scripserunt opera et fragmenta plurima nunc primum in lucem edita.* Paris, 1650.

Studies

Allard, G. H. "The Primacy of Existence in the Thought of Eriugena." In *Neoplatonism and Christian Thought*, ed. D. J. O'Meara, pp. 89–96. Albany, 1981.

Amann, E. "La controverse prédestinatienne." In *Histoire de l'église depuis les origines jusqu' à nos jours*, VI: *l'époque carolingienne*, ed. A. Fliche and V. Martin, pp. 320–44. Paris, 1947.

Brennan, M. "Materials for the Biography of Johannes Scottus Eriugena." *Studi medievali*, 3rd ser., 27:1 (1986): 413–60.

Cappuyns, M. *Jean Scot Érigène: sa vie, son oeuvre, sa pensée*. Louvain/Paris, 1933; reprint Brussels, 1964.

Contreni, J. J. "John Scottus, Martin Hiberniensis, the Liberal Arts and Teaching." In *Insular Latin Studies: Papers on Latin Texts and Manuscripts of the British Isles, 550–1066*, ed. M. Herren, pp. 23–44. Toronto, 1981.

Cristiani, M. "La notion de loi dans le 'De praedestinatione' de Jean Scot." In *Jean Scot Érigène et l'histoire de la philosophie*, pp. 277–88.

——. "'Lex-justitia': Giovanni Eriugena maestro palatino e la maturità della cultura carolingia," *Schede mediaevali*, 2 (1982): 14–31.

Devisse, J. *Hincmar archevêque de Rheims, 845–882*, vol. 1. Geneva, 1975.

D'Onofrio, G. "'Disputandi disciplina': procédés dialectiques et 'logica vetus' dans le langage philosophique de Jean Scot." In *Jean Scot écrivain*, ed. G.-H. Allard, pp. 229–63. Montreal/Paris, 1986.

——. *Fons Scientiae: la dialettica nell'Occidente tardoantico*. Naples, 1986.

Florus of Lyon. *Flori diaconi sub nomine ecclesiae lugdunensis aduersus Johannis Scoti Erigenae erroneas definitiones*. PL 119.101–250.

Ganz D. "The Debate on Predestination." In *Charles the Bald: Court and Kingdom*, ed. M. Gibson and J. Nelson, pp. 353–73. Oxford, 1981.

Gross, J. "Ur- und Erbsünde in der 'Physiologie' des Johannes Scotus Eriugena," *Zeitschrift für Kirchengeschichte*, 66:4 (1954–55): 254–71.

Jeauneau, E., ed. Jean Scot, *Homélie sur le Prologue de Jean*. Sources chrétiennes, number 151. Paris, 1969.

——. Jean Scot, *Commentaire sur l'Évangile de Jean*. Sources chrétiennes, number 180. Paris, 1972.

——. "Jean Scot Érigène et le grec," *Archivum latinitatis Medii Aevi*, 41 (1979): 5–50.

Lambon, C. *Oeuvres théologiques et grammaticales de Godescalc d'Orbais*. Louvain, 1945.

Bibliography

Lavaud, B. "Prédestination, IV: la controverse sur la prédestination au IXe siècle." In *Dictionnaire de théologie catholique,* ed. E. Amann, 12.2901–2935. Paris, 1933.

Liebeschütz, H. "Western Christian Thought from Boethius to Anselm." In *The Cambridge History of Later Greek and Early Medieval Philosphy,* ed. A. H. Armstrong, pp. 535–85. Cambridge, 1967.

———. "The Place of the Martianus *Glossae* in the Development of Eriugena's Thought." In *The Mind of Eriugena,* ed. J. J. O'Meara and L. Beiler, pp. 49–58. Dublin, 1973.

Madec, G. "L'augustinisme de Jean Scot dans le 'De praedestinatione.'" In *Jean Scot Érigène et l'histoire de la philosophie,* pp. 183–90.

Martello, C. *Simbolismo e Neoplatonismo in Giovanni Scoto Eriugena.* Symbolon. Studi e testi di filosofia antica e medievale, number 5. Catania, 1986.

Mathon, G. "L'utilisation des textes de Saint Augustin par Jean Scot Érigène dans son *De praedestinatione.*" In *Augustinus Magister: Actes du congrès international augustinien tenu à Paris, 21–24 septembre 1954,* vol. 3: 419–28. Paris, 1955.

Millosevich, F. "Giovanni Scoto Eriugena ed il significato del suo pensiero," *Sophia,* 6 (1938): 531–34.

Moran, D. *The Philosophy of John Scottus Eriugena: A Study of Idealism in the Middle Ages.* Cambridge, 1989.

O'Meara, D. J. "The Problem of Speaking about God in John Scottus Eriugena." In *Carolingian Essays: Andrew Mellon Lectures in Early Christian Studies,* ed. U.-R. Blumenthal, pp. 151–67. Washington, D.C., 1983.

O'Meara, J. J. *Eriugena.* Oxford, 1988.

Piemonte, G. "L'expression 'quae sunt et quae non sunt': Jean Scot et Marius Victorinus." In *Jean Scot écrivain,* ed. G.-H. Allard, pp. 81–113. Montreal/Paris, 1986.

Potesta, Gian Luca. "Ordine ed eresia nella controversia sull predestinazione." In *Giovanni Scoto nel suo tempo,* ed. C. Leonardi and E. Menestò, pp. 383–411. Spoleto, 1989.

Prudentius of Troyes. *Sancti Prudentii Trecensis episcopi de praedestinatione contra Joannem Scotum cognomento Erigenam.* PL 115.1009–1366.

Roques, R. "La symbolique de Jean Scot Érigène," *Annuaire de l'Ecole pratique des hautes etudes, Section des sciences religieuses: Annuaire, 1964–65,* pp. 121–25. Paris, 1964.

Russell, R. "Some Augustinian Influences in Eriugena's *De diuisione naturae.*" In *The Mind of Eriugena,* ed. J. J. O'Meara and L. Bieler, pp. 31–40 and 47. Dublin, 1973.

Schrimpf, G. "Die Sinnmite von '*Periphyseon,*'" In *Jean Scot Érigène et l'histoire de la philosophie,* pp. 327–36.

Bibliography

———. *Das Werk des Johannes Scottus Eriugena im Rahmen des Wissenschaftsverständnisses seiner Zeit: Eine Hinführung zu Periphyseon*. Beiträge zur Geschichte der Philosophie und Theologie des Mittelalters, Neue Folge, Band 23. Münster, 1982.

———. "Der Beitrag des Johannes Scottus Eriugena zum Prädestinationsstreit." In *Die Iren und Europa im früheren Mittelalter*, II, ed. H. Löwe, pp. 819–865. Stuttgart, 1982.

———. "Johannes Scottus Eriugena." In *Gestalten der Kirchengeschichte*, ed. M. Greschat, Bd. 3, pp. 113–22. Stuttgart, 1983.

Sheldon-Williams, I. P., "Eriugena's Greek Sources." In *The Mind of Eriugena*, ed. J. J. O'Meara and L. Bieler, pp. 1–14. Dublin, 1973.

———, ed. and trans. *Johannis Scotti Eriugenae Periphyseon ('De Diuisione Naturae') Liber Primus, Liber Secundus, Liber Tertius*. The Dublin Institute for Advanced Studies. Scriptores Latini Hiberniae. Vols. 7, 9, 11. Dublin, 1968–81.

Stock, B. "In Search of Eriugena's Augustine." *Eriugena: Studien zu seinen Quellen (Eriugena-Colloquium, Freiburg im Breisgau, August 1979)*, ed. W. Beierwaltes, pp. 85–104. Heidelberg, 1980.

Trouillard, J. "Proclos et Erigène: Quelques aspects de la théorie de l'âme," *Ecole pratique des hautes etudes, Ve section, sciences religieuses: Annuaire, 1968–69*, 76 (1968): 197–202.

———. "Rencontre du Néoplatonisme," *Revue de théologie et de philosophie*, 22 (1972): 1–13.

———. "Erigène et la théophanie créatrice." In *The Mind of Eriugena*, pp. 98–113.

———. "Métensomatose proclienne et eschatologie érigénienne." In *Philosophies non-chrétiennes et christianisme: Annales de l'Institut de Philosophie et de Sciences morales, 1984*, ed. J. Sojcher and G. Hottois, pp. 87–99. Brussels, 1984.

www.ingramcontent.com/pod-product-compliance
Lightning Source LLC
Chambersburg PA
CBHW022105160426
43198CB00008B/354